Onwards and Upwards

Onwards and Upwards

*Lessons from 10 Years Building
a Global Business*

or

The Blue Wireless Story

Ivan Landen

© 2026 Ivan Landen

All rights reserved: No part of this book may be reproduced in any form or by any means without permission in writing from the publisher, except by a reviewer who may quote brief passages in a review.

ISBN 9789090395586

First Edition

Contents

Foreword: Building Together 11
Foreword: From A Fellow Entrepreneur 17
Prologue 23
1   What is Your Dream? 31
    1.1   Building Your Dream 33
    1.2   Finding the Opportunity 35
    1.3   Getting Out There 38
    1.4   Choosing Lifestyle vs. Venture 41
    1.5   Your Product-Market Fit 43
2   The Right Team 49
    2.1   People make the difference 51
    2.2   The Founders 51
    2.3   The Right Staff 57
    2.4   The Right Investors 59
    2.5   The Early Supporters 67
    2.6   The Others 69
3   Surviving the Grind 73
    3.1   What is the Grind? 75
    3.2   Always be Closing 78
    3.3   Always be Promoting 84

	3.4	Always Be Evolving Your Brand	90
	3.5	Always be Hiring	100
	3.6	Always be Serving	104
	3.7	Always Keep Your Eye On The Money	108
4		Scaling to the Next Level	119
	4.1	The Next Phase	121
	4.2	The Business Strategy	122
	4.3	The Customer Journey	128
	4.4	The Global Expansion	132
	4.5	The Business Process	139
	4.6	The Automation	143
	4.7	People Make the Difference	147
5		Essential Skills	159
	5.1	Tools of the Trade	161
	5.2	Skill 1: Become Resilient	162
	5.3	Skill 2: Make Better Decisions	165
	5.4	Skill 3: Continuous Improvement	172
	5.5	Skill 4: Time Management	175
	5.6	Skill 5: Endless Creativity	179
6		The Art of the Exit	191
	6.1	Why Sell?	193
	6.2	Four Ways to Sell a Business	197
	6.3	How Much is enough?	198

6.4	Determining the Right Time	200
6.5	Selling for the First Time	202
6.6	Closing the Deal	208
6.7	The Earn-Out	211
7	We Made It!	215
7.1	Life Changing?	217
7.2	Expansion Continues	219
7.3	More Growth and Complexity	226
7.4	Leaders create leaders	227
8	What I Have Learned	233
9	Thank You	239
10	References	247

Foreword: Building Together

By Joop Gerlach, Co-founder Blue Wireless

I remember the first time I met Ivan. It was in 1998 in Amsterdam, and we were both working in the booming telecommunications industry at a company called Infonet. While Ivan was based in the Netherlands office and I was at the regional office, you somehow always seem to filter out and connect with those people in a company who are a bit different—special. Ivan is one of those standouts, both on a personal and a business level.

We worked in different parts of the business and had very different skill sets. I was a technical consultant, helping customers with their network needs. Ivan was in sales and marketing. We struck up a friendship and had great fun, but we could also work seriously when needed—and that's where we first clicked. I would send him what I was thinking and, voilà, twenty minutes later I'd have a fully developed PowerPoint presentation in my inbox. Amazing.

While we each followed our own careers over the next 17 years, taking us all over the globe, when Ivan pitched the idea of starting a business in late 2015, it didn't take me long to say yes. Reality settled in quickly, as starting a business from scratch is not easy. Like Ivan, I had a family with kids in school and an established lifestyle after a successful career in the global telco industry, so being without income for the first time was daunting. Having the support of my wife and children was essential to the success we achieved. My wife has always been my biggest fan, but after I mortgaged the house for the third time, she regularly reminded me: "We're not going to lose the house, right?" When we successfully exited Blue Wireless, she said, "You did it!"—to which I replied, "No, we did it."

This book provides key insights into the journey of being a founder, and let me tell you: it is one hell of an emotional rollercoaster. My father-in-law used to say, "You can't experience highs if you don't experience lows," and I can confirm how true that is. That's where the special relationship between Ivan and me comes in. We both went through our own ups and downs, and we were able to motivate ourselves—and each other—when it mattered most. I recall one time when I was feeling particularly down and Ivan sent me a meme of a Paralympic swimmer with no arms or legs, captioned: "And you think you have problems??" It snapped me right out of it and lifted me when I needed it most. I also loved our Blue Wireless playlist, with songs like 'Don't Stop Believing', 'Stressed Out', and 'I'm Still Standing', just to name a few. Enough to get our mental focus back, return to the grind, and keep going.

Clearly, starting a business is hard—and as Ivan describes in this book, doing it alone is impossible. You become completely dependent on each other, and even our families became intertwined with the business. Both of my sons worked for Blue Wireless with absolute commitment, never resting until a project was done. One such test came during a project for a customer in Australia in the hospitality business, Scape Student Living. On the day of installation, the elevators were out of service. Rather than cancelling, we climbed 29 floors by stairs with all our equipment—not once, but at least ten times up and down until the job was done. As a dad, I couldn't be more proud of my boys and one later confessed that what he disliked most was the 'desk' part of the job.

But it wasn't just Ivan, me, or our families who worked hard. Along the way, we built a fantastic team without whom none of this would have been possible. An amazing group of people—globally dispersed and representing over 30 nationalities. They were, and still are, a great source of motivation for us.

Did Ivan and I always agree in business? Hell no. Although surprisingly limited, we did have a few shouting matches when one of us was being too stubborn or overreaching in our respective area of responsibility. But even when we disagreed, we knew our shared motivation: we wanted the business to succeed. So we didn't dwell on it—we moved on. And if a decision turned out to be wrong, we worked together to minimise the damage.

Reading this book won't give you all the answers on how to succeed in starting a business, nor will it prevent you from making the same mistakes we made. You will—and you should. But it does offer valuable insights that can help prepare you for the pitfalls along the way and provides plenty of lessons learned.

My key advice is simple: don't do it alone. We were lucky that Ivan and I share the same outlook on life and business while being highly complementary in our skills. That made all the difference—and made this journey one of the best experiences of my life.

Would I do it again? Absolutely.

Onwards and Upwards.

Foreword: From a Fellow Entrepreneur

by Oliver Tucker, CEO Wireless Logic Group

I have read many books about entrepreneurship over the years. Few have felt as familiar as this one.

When Wireless Logic acquired Blue Wireless, we were not just buying a business—we were recognising a journey that closely mirrored our own. Reading Ivan's account of building Blue Wireless brought back vivid memories of the early days of Wireless Logic: the conviction that wireless would fundamentally reshape connectivity, the grind of turning belief into execution, and the quiet resilience required to build something long before the market fully understands what you are doing.

What Ivan describes so candidly in these pages is the reality of building a company from first principles. The long stretches of progress that go unnoticed. The decisions made with incomplete information. The necessity of backing your judgement when there is no playbook to follow. These are experiences every founder recognises, regardless of geography, scale, or outcome.

What makes this book particularly compelling is its honesty. Ivan does not romanticise entrepreneurship, nor does he attempt to reduce it to frameworks or formulas. Instead, he shares the emotional and practical realities of building a business: the trade-offs, the doubts, the moments of quiet satisfaction when something finally works. That authenticity is rare, and it is what makes this story so valuable.

This is not a book about winning fast or thinking big for the sake of it. It is about building properly—with care for customers, respect for people, and an understanding that meaningful businesses are shaped over time, not overnight.

Those principles are ones we strongly believe in, and they are evident throughout Ivan's journey.

Ivan's story is not a how-to guide, nor does it pretend there is a single right way to build a company. Instead, it offers something far more valuable: perspective. Ivan recounts the realities of entrepreneurship with humility, clarity, and an appreciation for both the highs and the inevitable lows. For anyone considering starting a business—or already deep into the journey—this is a refreshingly grounded and reassuring read.

Entrepreneurship is often portrayed as glamorous. In truth, it is demanding, uncertain, and deeply personal. But as Ivan's story shows—and as we have experienced ourselves—it is also immensely rewarding when done with purpose, integrity, and perseverance.

Reading this book reminded me just how universal the founder experience really is. No matter how a company ultimately evolves, the early years leave a permanent mark—the responsibility you feel for your people, the weight of decisions that sit with you long after the day ends, and the quiet satisfaction that comes from seeing something you once imagined become real. Ivan captures that experience with clarity and humility, and in doing so, offers reassurance to every founder that the doubts, the pressure, and the persistence are not signs of weakness—they are simply part of the journey.

I am proud that Blue Wireless is now part of the Wireless Logic story. Even more so, I am pleased that Ivan has chosen to share his.

Onwards and upwards.

Prologue

"Do you want to leave?"

"Do you want to leave?" That simple question, asked in a small meeting room in Amsterdam during the summer of 2015, set the wheels in motion for the greatest adventure of my life—starting my own company.

After years in international business, I was the managing director for the Asia Pacific region at a global internet service provider called Expereo. On paper, I'd reached a point in my career that some might envy. But inside I was restless and unhappy. The company I worked for had grown from a small team in the Netherlands into a global business, and the founders were preparing to sell the company to a private equity firm and exit the business. For the founders, it was the natural conclusion to years of hard work. For me, it was a signal that my time as a corporate employee had to end.

Up to that point, my career had followed a steady trajectory up the corporate ladder. After graduating in economics in Amsterdam in 1995, I wanted to get into international business and found a great sales role at the Dutch branch of an American telecommunications firm called Infonet. It was the '90s—an incredible time to start a career. I had a great boss (Harry van Streun, who later became my business mentor), plenty of travel, constant learning, and great pay.

Those years were full of opportunities, including one that took me to Asia. In 1999, I moved to Singapore to join a newly launched telco called StarHub. The job was more product and domestically focused, but being in the "little red dot" of Southeast Asia gave new perspective and opened new doors across the region. Two years later, I was offered the chance to lead the Thai branch of Infonet—the same American company I had started with in the

Netherlands. And so, in 2001, I moved to Thailand, where I found myself the only foreigner in the office and discovered that thirty of the thirty-five staff did not speak English (and I did not speak Thai!).

The posting in Thailand was a crash course in running a business—and in learning about myself. It was the first time I was truly responsible as "the boss" and foreshadowed a little of what I would encounter later with Blue Wireless. When I moved into a regional role for Infonet in the Asia Pacific, it was a relief: a more corporate environment with more structure and professionalism.

The following decade brought several more regional roles, travel, and a whirlwind of life events: I met my wife, started a family, and eventually moved back to Singapore to begin the next chapter at Expereo.

Expereo was also the first time I worked with true founders—people who had the guts to put everything on the line and build something from scratch. One of them was Walter Brunink, an old colleague from my early days at Infonet in the Netherlands, where he'd worked in the finance department. Everyone knew Walter as a nice, down-to-earth, hardworking guy who knew every detail of the business; he was not a flashy sales champion or engineering genius—just a quiet, relentless worker. I now recognize that he had exactly the temperament needed to be a successful founder.

As Walter and the team went through their exit process, I was standing on the sidelines. By early 2015, the corporate environment at Expereo had become increasingly constrained for me. With the company preparing for sale, new initiatives became scarce and the room for innovation disappeared. My leadership style—direct and sometimes unconventional—met growing resistance, and I found myself increasingly at odds with senior management. It became clear that my ambitions were no longer aligned with the company's direction.

So, when the question "Do you want to leave?" was asked at a meeting in Amsterdam, it came as no surprise. Nor was it a hard decision. Yes—it was time to go. The timing felt right, and in many ways, it was a relief.

By then, my confidence had grown: not the polished corporate kind but a quieter sense that I could start something bare bones and make it work. I could do it.

I didn't want to just continue and look for the next job without ever scratching that itch. Even Jeff Bezos has publicly described leaving a lucrative Wall Street job because he feared regretting *not* trying.

Later that day, I sat my wife down, took her hands, and asked, "Do you trust me?" Puzzled, she said, "Uh, yes, of course…what's happening?" I told her I'd resigned.

"You did what?!" she yelled. Once I calmed her down, I explained my "grand plan"—to start my own business. Of course, that initial plan was incredibly naïve compared to what would actually unfold, but I had a few months of paid garden leave, an incentive payout, and some savings. Financially, it felt manageable, and emotionally, I was ready to take on the world. It was summer in the Netherlands—the season for optimism—and we were ready for a break.

The excitement of leaving corporate life did not last long. When we returned to Singapore after the summer, reality hit. Singapore is one of the most expensive cities in the world, and we'd been living very comfortably. Our colonial bungalow rental alone cost around 10,000 Singapore dollars per month. We had car payments, a live-in maid, international school fees, and an expat lifestyle—not exactly ideal conditions for bootstrapping a startup.

It was a sobering experience but also clarifying. It forced me to think hard about what really mattered. Yes, we had to move out of that bungalow and downsize the car, but despite many more sacrifices, there hasn't been a single day when I've regretted that decision. The experience was also transformational—like becoming a parent for the first time. If you have that gnawing feeling inside that says, "I can do this better," I'd recommend taking the leap.

* * *

With the ten-year anniversary celebration of Blue Wireless behind us, it feels fitting to put it all together—the history, the lessons, and the mistakes—in one story that might help other aspiring entrepreneurs, early-stage founders, or those who are trying to scale towards an exit. Whether you are leaving behind a corporate career, starting fresh from university, or launching a business later in life, the challenges and opportunities are remarkably similar.

Blue Wireless investors, staff, customers, and partners will hopefully get a chuckle when reading this book. What were these guys thinking? Was there any method to the madness? Many will recognize the many events described, although I certainly have forgotten several. So much has happened over ten years.

Looking back now, it has been the adventure of a lifetime. Entrepreneurship isn't a straight line; it is a series of decisions, each building on the last, each shaping the future of your business. Blue Wireless has grown far beyond what I imagined, and despite the hard work and scary moments, it has been immense fun. We built something meaningful, made friends across the world, and created memories that will last forever.

So here it is—my attempt to write down what I've learned from those early days through the grind, the scaling, the selling, and beyond. This isn't a full start-up manual or business textbook. It is just my story, told as honestly as possible with some lessons along the way.

And, if you are ready for your own adventure, take a deep breath and hold onto the words that guided us through it all: "Onwards and upwards."

1 What is Your Dream?

Fortune favors the bold.

1.1 Building Your Dream

A lot of wonderful things have been said about entrepreneurship: the freedom, the flexibility, the financial rewards, the control of your destiny. But if it were really that easy and great, everyone would be doing it, right?

It is a big ask to dream, and an even bigger one to turn that dream into reality. Most of us are already consumed by daily routines—work, family, responsibilities—and those are challenging enough to navigate. Who has time to dream about a future vision on top of that? Dreaming feels like a luxury we cannot afford, especially when life is hectic, stressful, or financially tight.

But the opposite is also true: When everything is going well and life feels comfortable, who wants to risk it all to start something new, stressful, and uncertain?

I was in that second category. By 2015, I had worked over twenty years in global telecommunications companies—or "telcos"—climbing steadily from account manager to regional managing director. It had been a rewarding career: good pay, international travel, prestige. I could easily have continued another ten or fifteen years and worked my way up to any C-level.

So, what made me risk that comfort—and my family's stability—to start over? Was it about making money? Or something deeper? What was driving me? What was I trying to prove, and to whom?

I guess every entrepreneur has a different driver. Some want to win. Some want recognition. Some want wealth. For some it only becomes clear during the journey.

For me, I learned along the way that my main drivers were curiosity and the desire to create things: a constant urge to figure out how things work, discover new things, and make them my own.

Looking back to my childhood, that factor had always been there: building endlessly with LEGO, constructing forts outside in the summer, inventing silly contraptions indoors in the winter. When the '80s came along, I was the first one with a computer. From a ZX81 (in black and white) to the Commodore 64 (color, woo-hoo!) to a Macintosh to the XT clones, I loved all of it: downloaded computer programs from the radio (yes, that was a thing, Google it) and swapped cassettes tapes with other kids. I was never a real coder beyond BASIC, but nerd enough to make everything work.

Then as a teenager, my curiosity meant exploring lots of different music genres and branches of science—as an adult, travel and cultures. Always moving, always exploring, always straying off the beaten path.

I love building and solving things, but I never had the patience to be a real engineer. For me, an 80 percent success rate felt good enough—time to move on to the next challenge. So, surely not good enough to be a doctor or a rocket scientist; people would die.

For me, starting a business was a personal challenge: Could I do it? Did I have what it takes? Could I build something bigger than myself? That curiosity and creative drive fueled me through the ten years of building Blue Wireless, from start to finish.

I wanted to build something—and discover things along the way. Now I just needed the right idea.

1.2 Finding the Opportunity

To understand the opportunity that led to the creation of Blue Wireless, it helps to know the segment of the telecommunications industry where I spent most of my career: corporate network services.

Corporate networks are private communication networks used by global companies—their own "private internet"—connecting offices and business systems so employees can work, and data can flow securely. These networks are the invisible backbone of global companies like DHL, Korean Air, or Nestlé, enabling factories, deliveries, bookings, production, accounting, and so forth and connecting their applications, computers, data centers, and more.

The global networks that make this possible were built and maintained by global service providers (GSPs) in the '80s and '90s. Those networks relied on a vast web of undersea cables rolled out during that period, and GSPs would have a point-of-presence of their network in almost every developed country in the world. But the difficult part in connecting the local offices of their global customers to those points-of-presence was the *local* connection—the "last mile." Local telecommunications companies were responsible for this portion and being legacy or state controlled in many countries meant that they were often too slow, too expensive, or too unreliable.

This was the "Achilles' heel" of the business model and sometimes the "last mile" connection would be more expensive than the international connection—similar to international travel, where in some cities you can pay more for the local taxi ride than the international flight to get to that city.

By the early 2000s, things were changing fast due to the boom of the internet and the new Internet access options that were developing fast, mostly fueled by residential broadband. As dial-up phone lines changed to ASDL and then fiber connections, consumers gained access to faster connectivity at lower prices.

But global corporate network services were slow to adopt, struggling with the different standards globally and the early unreliability of the internet.

That is where Expereo, a start-up from the Netherlands, saw an opportunity when they started in 2004. Their proposition was simple but powerful: contract the best local internet providers in every country around the world, aggregate them globally, and resell their services to GSPs. Think of it like booking hotels through Booking.com—clear pricing, reliable service, and access to options that weren't visible before. Expereo's approach to the "aggregation" of local Internet access revolutionized the network services industry and massively improved options and lowered prices for GSPs and corporate customers.

When I joined Expereo in 2012, the business model was already proven, and the business was growing rapidly. But like any growing company, choices had to be made about new opportunities and emerging technologies.

One of these technologies was "mobile internet"—or 3G—which was transforming the consumer world during that same time. The Apple iPhone had been around for several years and smartphones were taking over the legacy Nokias from the previous decade.

But while consumers and individual business users were massively using mobile internet, for corporate connectivity, it was too early. The reality was that 3G service was still too slow, patchy, and unreliable for access to global networks. Expereo tried some implementations, but despite lots of patience and technical experimentation, it did not meet customer expectations.

By 2015, the next generation of mobile connectivity had arrived: LTE (long-term evolution), better known as 4G. It offered faster speeds and, more importantly, a roadmap to 5G—a truly wireless future.

Still scarred by the poor experience of using 3G, Expereo's leadership decided to wait. The "wired" business was proven and business was booming. But from my perspective, with nothing to lose or protect, I saw something different. My lightbulb moment: Use 4G for corporate Internet access.

Everywhere I looked, the world was going wireless—phones, remotes, speakers, laptops. It felt inevitable that business connectivity would follow. The idea stuck with me like a splinter in my brain. I couldn't stop thinking about it.

When I rambled about a "wireless future" to people, the response was lukewarm at best. This was something for the "consumer" business, with phones and mobile plans, nothing for us in the "corporate" network space. But the more they doubted, the more convinced I became. I fully believed that wireless connectivity would become a mainstream solution for corporate networks. That conviction became the seed for starting Blue Wireless.

1.3 Getting Out There

On August 20, 2015, it officially started. With my passport, a check for 1,000 Singapore dollars, and the name "Blue Wireless" (more about that later) in my head, I went to register the company in Singapore. Blue Wireless Pte. Ltd. was born.

In the weeks that followed, I immersed myself in the Singapore start-up scene—networking events, investor pitches, endless coffee chats. It was a fascinating crowd: some sharp, some less so, but all full of dreams. I visited incubators, venture capitalists, coworking spaces, family offices, fireside chats, and more hip events.

But I quickly realized my idea—"wireless internet access for corporates"—did not exactly light up the room. Investors were chasing artificial intelligence, crypto, and augmented reality. I was the corporate expat pitching something that sounded…boring.

After two months of talking and listening, it became clear to me: No one really cares about your start-up. Everyone's too busy chasing their own needs and their own dreams. And among start-up founders, you are not competitors nor collaborators—you are just on separate journeys.

That was the first big lesson: Focus on yourself, your business, your customers. Listen to others, get feedback, but do not let them distract you from your journey or get lost in the noise. It is like training in a gym: People around you might inspire or give advice or look more buff, fat, or scrawny—it doesn't matter in the end; you must lift your own weights.

And with that, lesson number two followed: Just get started. Getting started is the biggest mental block because you worry about all the things you lack: your product isn't ready, you have no reputation, no staff, no customers. Forget that. The best thing you can do is simply *start*.

And an important portion of getting started is getting into a real office. Time to move out of the spare bedroom and establish something that feels like a business.

The first registered office location for Blue Wireless was on Robinson Road in Singapore in a coworking office called JustCo. While most freelancers and consultants were working in the common areas, I choose to rent one of the private offices. While it was three times the rate of a public desk, my pride insisted on having a place with my own logo at the door, and when it was affixed a week later, I was as proud as a peacock. I was a real business! Of course, I hadn't sold a thing and achieved anything yet, but the routine of dressing up, going to the office, and working in the central business district area put me in the right mindset for the things to come.

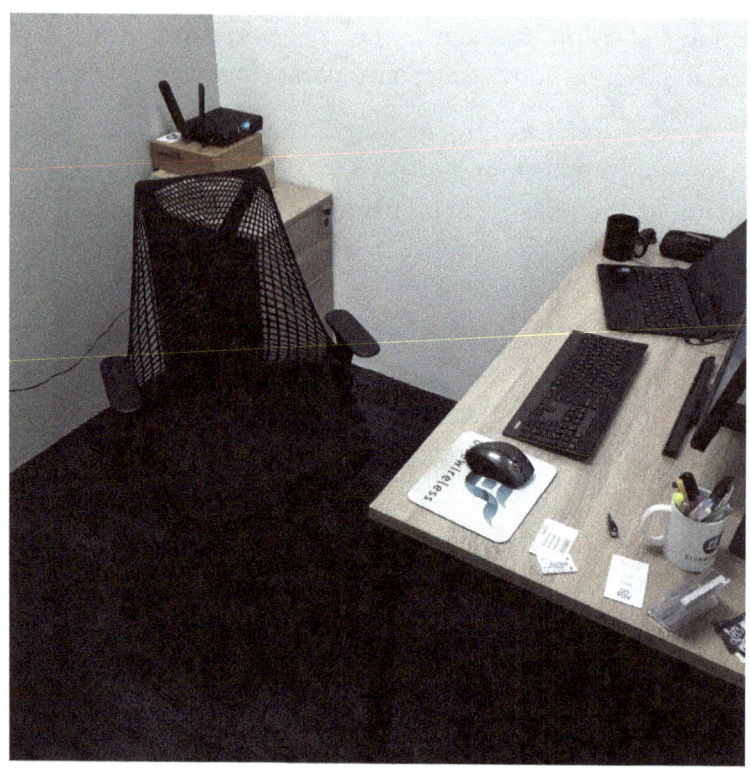

The first office on Robinson Road, Singapore, 2016

My wife came to visit the week after and was a bit puzzled to see why I was so excited, as the office was literally the size of a janitor's closet with no window. Many years later, she confided in me that she cried back in the car after she had left the office, comparing it to the corporate offices I had enjoyed in previous jobs and worrying that I had made the wrong choice with this career change—but I was oblivious to it.

1.4 Choosing Lifestyle vs. Venture

Building a business is an endless series of decision-making, and one of the key decisions that you need to make early on is about the type of business you want to build.

I'm not talking about what legal form (whether private limited or partnership, etc.) but fundamentally how ambitious you want to get. In the start-up literature, this is called the difference between a lifestyle business and a venture business. Let me explain.

- A lifestyle business is a business that you can build and manage with the purpose to create immediate value for yourself and maybe your family. Value comes in many forms: financially in your salary and dividends and of course in your enjoyment of running the business and potentially building something for your family, if you are thinking about succession. If you are starting a bed and breakfast, a surf school, or a consultancy practice, you are likely building a lifestyle business.
- A venture business is a business that is created with the purpose of generating value for future investors, and by exiting this business, you can convert this value into a payout for yourself. The enjoyment comes from the creating and building. You will have to pay yourself, but you must keep in the back of your mind that the ultimate goal is to create value for a future investor.

You can compare it with an expedition to a mountain top where you prepare, climb, and eventually reach the top, to follow with a decent for potentially a next adventure to another mountain top. Such an expedition is a very different endeavor than when your goal is to live in the hills, building your home, and retiring there.

This is an important distinction to make at the beginning, as along the way you will have to not only identify the right customers, staff, and suppliers—like in any business—but you will also have to start defining who will be the potential purchasers of your company.

Early on in Blue Wireless, I decided that my purpose was to build a business, grow it large enough, and sell it. Why? Of course, I was inspired by the usual success stories, such as Mark Zuckerberg and Steve Jobs (although they did not exit and sell their businesses). But again, I was driven by the challenge. I had little ambition to just start a small business that I could work in until retirement, such as a coffee shop, or work as a consultant for hire, which really is not a business but just a different employment strategy. I wanted to build a real business with multiple offices, lots of staff, global customers—the whole shebang.

At that time, I was still more naïve, and I promised my wife that "I'll give myself a year and if it doesn't work out, I'll go back to a regular job." Personally, I had set the target around two to three years, calculating that I might be able to financially stretch that far. And since the Expereo founders had done it in ten years, I should be able to do it much faster, right?

Of course this was incredibly naïve at the time, as one, two, or even three years is far too short to accomplish anything of scale.

If your ambition is to build a lifestyle business, to become a successful consultant or retailer, it might be possible, but even in those types of businesses, it takes longer and costs more than initially imagined.

But besides the need for time and money, what I also learned from my previous months while I was immersed in the start-up culture and literature was the need for "the right offering for the right market." This is also better known as "product-market fit."

1.5 Your Product-Market Fit

A "product-market fit" (or product-market combination) refers to the specific proposition (product or service) you want to offer to the specific market segment (target audience). Many business school textbooks have elaborated on this topic, talking about stars and cash cows and dogs, market expansion versus market extension, product breadth versus niche focus, etc.

Simply put, your product-market combination is basically what you sell to whom, and the more specific and unique you can make your product offer and the more precise you can define your customer within the market, the more successful you will be. And as your business evolves, you will have to constantly evaluate and refine this combination, as it is essential to your long-term success.

My advice for any new entrepreneur is simple: Only start a venture business in an industry and market that you already know. This is a must, a nonnegotiable.

The world is full of stories of failed entrepreneurs who started something new in a field that they were completely not familiar with. Been an engineer for twenty years and opening a bar? Probably a bad idea—unless you do not mind losing money. Worked in the fitness industry and now want to get into renewable energy? Forget it. Just thinking about "inventing" a product without a market? Do not even think about it. Yes, you can do it as a lifestyle business but not as a venture business, because you'll run out of time and money before you can create sufficient value to sustain the business or sell it.

When I started Blue Wireless, I had been active in the network services industry for a good twenty years, building up a good understanding of the customers, their buying behaviors, the vendors, the technical developments, and so forth. But besides understanding the customer side, I had a network of people built over the years. This network turned out to be one of the pillars of success through the different stages as I was looking for customers, suppliers, investors, and staff to hire. The majority of those came from my existing industry network.

And, while you do need good insight into the development of markets—like how I had identified the rise of wireless technologies for corporate networks—you do not need some groundbreaking invention or magic idea. The era of "inventors" is over; nobody is looking for a better mousetrap.

What you do need is a keen desire to improve things and an "angle" on the market that you should already know and ideally one where people in the market know you. Or you can anticipate the developments in the market: So what is up and coming in your specific field or industry. As the dad of Wayne Gretzky, the great Canadian ice hockey player put it: "Skate to where the puck is going to be, not where it is." (He also said: "You miss 100 percent of the shots you don't take," which is another great advice for any entrepreneur.)

But back to starting in an industry you know, here are two examples of friends who did the same and exited successfully.

One of my good friends from Bangkok worked for a US company selling chemical additives in the Asia Pacific, supplying the world's largest producers of consumer plastics and fully learning the complex supply chain that industrial plastic production involves. As the market for plastics evolved and consumers put more emphasis on materials that are safe, durable, and protective, he started his own brand in the market for antimicrobial additives, capitalizing on the knowledge and contacts he had built up during his career. He successfully sold and exited his company ten years later to a global market leader in the industry.

One other friend worked in shrimp farming for a decade, fully understanding the complexities of industrial seafood farming and the complex supply chain of fresh food distribution. As the market evolved and consumers demanded more luxury fresh fish products, he embarked on building a premium-branded seafood business, supplying retailers and restaurants. Over a period of ten years, the business grew exponentially, eventually dominating the segment of premium fresh seafood imports, and he was able to sell a significant portion of the business to a larger industry player.

Both capitalized on their existing knowledge and long-term trends, not temporary fads. Both built their companies during the same period I was building Blue Wireless, and both sold their businesses successfully to new investors.

The learning curve is already very steep when starting a business; if you do this in an industry that is new to you, you will increase your risk of failure exponentially. So, to repeat my advice: Stick to your industry

The second part of the product-market combination is that you clearly define your unique offering within that market for the specific customer segment and what specific need you are addressing. What problems are you solving? Or in case of consumers, what desire or want you are satisfying?

Early on at Blue Wireless, we made a choice to focus on the niche of "wireless internet access for corporates." Now, for those not in the industry, this might seem already quite specific, until you realize that both segments are multi-billion dollar markets by itself. So you have to further drill down and make it even more specific: which country, which specific industries within the corporate segment, which technology, complex or simple requirements, what type of customer buying behavior, etc. The fine-tuning of a proposition is something that is ongoing and will need to be adjusted every few months as you progress.

There are enough business books that tell you to do market research to ensure you know how large the market is and then target a percentage, but in my experience, this is a seldom useful guideline. I have seen enough presentations from naïve entrepreneurs who put statements on their slides about capturing 5 percent of some billion-dollar market. So what? Most markets are so huge, the total size is irrelevant for a starting entrepreneur. It's more important is to answer who your specific customer is and what your unique proposition is, and the more specific and unique you can make it, the better.

Now, there are tons of reasons why start-ups fail and enough literature and articles about it, but most of those are about the execution later in the process. Start with the basic questions of what is your mission and what is your purpose as a business, translate that to a product-market combination, and then get started!

Key Learnings

- *Start a business around your passion—something fascinating, challenging, and rewarding. Money cannot be the primary motivation.*
- *Decide early whether you are building a lifestyle or a venture business—many future decisions depend on it.*
- *Only start in a market you know, and define a clear, evolving product-market combination.*
- *Get out there, learn, fill your knowledge gaps, and refine your proposition.*
- *Most importantly: Just get started.*

2 THE RIGHT TEAM

If you want to go fast, go alone.
If you want to go far, go together.

2.1 People make the difference

Of the many lessons I have learned during the years at Blue Wireless, the following is a big one: You cannot build a business alone. But this is not just about hiring the right staff, which is a huge task by itself. You need a full support system of people who back you in your mission, from investors, early adopters, suppliers, friends, and family. And as the company evolves and grows, so does your team as well—it's all part of the journey.

In the next few sections, I'll share the main learnings around finding (and keeping) the right people for your business, including the founders, staff, investors, and supporters.

2.2 The Founders

A few weeks after that actual moment of registering Blue Wireless, it dawned on me that I needed a business partner, someone who could not only complement my skills and experience but also someone who I could share the ups and downs of the business with—someone on equal footing, similar in outlook in life and business.

Choosing a partner in a business is make or break and very much like a marriage. If you are marrying the wrong person, you can still have a family, but the chances of failure are much larger, and you will probably have a miserable time. And similar to a marriage, you do not know up front how the person will turn out in the long run; you will only find out afterwards…

I got extremely lucky not just with the woman I married but also my business partner and cofounder of Blue Wireless: Joop Gerlach.

Joop started out around the same time in 2015 on his own and at that time was providing information and communication technology services and consultancy in Australia under the name Gerlach Telecom. Joop and I had been friends for close to twenty years at that point, bumping into each other every few years as colleagues and suppliers at various organizations as we moved between companies and countries. We always had a good time when we got together at industry conferences or events, sharing the same passion for gin and tonics—and we shared many in Singapore, Bangkok, and Hong Kong, to name a few.

But alcohol-fueled discussions at the bar about "how to conquer the world" eventually turned into more serious discussions on business.

Many talks followed about the latest network technology, our frustrations about the corporate world, and the flawed decision-making we saw in the large organizations that we worked for or tried to sell to. And then the discussions started about ambition: What if? How could we do it better? When?

Once you get serious, the hardest part of those discussions are the points on who does what and who gets what, but we approached it, probably unknowingly, similar to a marriage.

Joop and I during one of the many Hong Kong Sevens we attended.

We went in full in as equals, both put up funds, both worked full time, and both realized that one could not do it without the other. We regularly adjusted our roles and expectations as things evolved and had those conversations about who does what or—the more difficult—who would stop certain work or give up certain responsibilities.

Giving up things or letting go of things is usually the hardest part for any entrepreneur because you cling on to control as much as you can, thinking you have the right ideas, plans, skills, or work ethic to make it successful. (More about letting go in future chapters.) But since we used the approach of *winning together or failing together* from the start, it was fundamental in building an even bigger team where both Joop and I are the founding pillars.

Our first Cradlepoint award, Boise, Idaho, 2017

Any comparison with famous entrepreneurs who founded giants like Google or Microsoft are dangerous, but it is striking how many of those were started by people who complemented each other: Steve Wozniak wanted to implement elegant engineering; Steve Jobs wanted to build a company that changed the world—completely different temperaments. Apple exists because both sides were needed, and the same is true for Blue Wireless; it would not exist without the balancing skills and personalities that Joop and I brought together.

A portion that many founders struggle with is share ownership, and there are multiple perspectives here to consider as shares represent both control in the business and future financial reward.

To start with the latter, yes, starting with a cofounder feels like "giving up" half of your business, and you know that in the event of an exit, your proceeds could have been double or more. This hurts, but there is little point arguing about it, because if your business would fail, it doesn't matter whether you own it partly or fully: 100 percent of zero is still zero. Our key objective at this stage was to increase the chances of business success, and for us it was a clear winning combination.

On the shares, we settled around a 53-to-47 split, which was simply based on the amount of money we contributed to the first "funding round" of roughly 100,000 Singapore dollars each.

Many more funding rounds were to follow in subsequent years as we needed to raise money from external investors, leading to the feared "dilution." For founders, it is life or death to keep your ownership above 50 percent and the rows closed as cofounders so you can remain in ultimate control of your business. There are enough cases where entrepreneurs effectively got locked out of their own business. Even Steve Jobs was fired by his own board from Apple at the early stage…(but of course made a miraculous comeback).

As you progress, investors, staff, and others will continue to ask for more shares or options, and these you must manage carefully. Especially it is important to understand what is it what they are really after: reward or control? For staff, it is usually about reward, to compensate for the low salary and risk of working at a start-up. So giving more shares can solve that, but often there are more suitable options, such as stock options.

For investors, it is reward, but stocks are also a method of control, to help protect their investment. Similarly, there are often more appropriate tools to achieve that, for instance through guarantees or regular payments.

Next to shared ownership, the directorship is the other element you need to define between founders, as directors effectively control the day-to-day business. For us, it was simple: two directors, and both had equal "rights" to make decisions.

But besides these formal aspects of shares and directorship, the most important element between founders is having trust and that requires a radical honesty and openness, again, akin to marriage.

We set up things like systems and logins in a way that there was little room nor incentive to cheat, with full visibility. For example, for many years, we used the same passwords for systems and could see anything either of us did anytime. Probably more open than most marriages!

2.3 The Right Staff

The line between founders and staff is blurry in the beginning, but once you start interviewing and talking about salaries and employment contracts, rather than shares or investments, you know it is different.

Up to that time, Joop and myself actually did not even have an employment contract, and I paid myself the minimum to keep my employment pass active in Singapore. During the first years, our salary was certainly not enough to pay for normal family expenses, and we effectively lived off our savings. After those were depleted, we used the various personal loans that we accumulated along the way.

Hiring your first staff is a difficult task, as you have little to show for as a business, and you can only offer limited salary to prospective employees. And besides that, most staff are not looking only for salary but also seeking security, process, colleagues, career development, and more—all things that we couldn't offer on day one.

While we did try to use the "start-up" angle to woo prospective candidates, for some this had the adverse result, as it invoked conceptions about a crazy, hip office with a giant slide and cool foam parties—all things that we certainly did not have day one. In fact, the reality was more depressing. Our first office had two desks, no windows, and most of the time we were working in the pantry area.

How about shares, stock options, and promises of future riches? That was also a tough one, since certainly at the beginning of Blue Wireless we did not know how big the business could be, so financial expectations were modest. And Joop and I had only just come to terms with our own share reduction/dilution from partnering, so giving up even further shares early on was difficult.

So, what can you offer your first staff? Purpose and comradery. It is not much and sounds cliché, but what I learned about most people, and myself, is that we want to work on something that is worthwhile, together in a place where our contribution makes a difference and is appreciated.

So right from the start—before we had properly written down any business mission and vision statements—we brought our belief and enthusiasm for our business and appreciation and solidarity for all staff, which made a difference in attracting people to the business and keeping them engaged. We practiced what we preached, lived by our values, and "ate our own dog food" when it came to using wireless for everything possible in the business. We kept this practice as the business and the number of staff continued to grow.

Over the ten years that followed, Blue Wireless hired over two hundred staff and fired close to fifty—and almost all I've been personally involved in. Without a doubt, being able to attract, keep, and let go staff is a skill that is essential for every entrepreneur. More about this in the chapter on scaling the business.

But if you think finding staff is hard, get ready for the second group of people that are make or break for any start-up company: investors.

2.4 THE RIGHT INVESTORS

If you are starting a business, you need money, much more money than you think you do. Even if you are an expert at accounting and cash flow planning, I guarantee you will underestimate the ongoing need for ever more cash. Not surprisingly, the number one reason why successful start-up businesses fail is cash flow issues. Not for lack of good ideas, customers, or hard work, but it's simply underestimating the amount of money you keep on needing and receiving in time, especially once your business is growing and starting to get successful.

Money could be a chapter by itself, and tons of books have been written about it, from raising to managing to accounting to valuations. But I'm putting it first under the people section, as the money you likely need early on will come from people: people who you know, new ones you need to find, and those you need to convince and ultimately whose trust you need to win.

So, where to start? Well, the list is long, and we tried every possible angle.

Government Grants

Ah, the government... Naïve as we were, we thought there must be some "funding" waiting for us, right? Stimulate new business, support young entrepreneurs, and so on, but we quickly found out that for most attempts, it was a dead end.

Either they were for specific sectors not related to ours or required lengthy qualification processes that would take months. In the Singapore context, most were reserved for Singapore citizens, and with Joop and me as founders we were considered "foreign" shareholders.

Of course, this depends on the country, but even if you are successful in securing some initial funds, these programs will be limited, and there is little chance you can go for multiple "rounds" in government programs. So, it's a nice boost, and take it if you can, but it cannot be a long-term strategy.

We did receive some nice handouts later during the Covid-19 period, but in my experience, government funding was not a reliable source.

Bank Loans

Commercial or banking loans are usually the second area entrepreneurs look at, but for us, this was also a very limited source.

As a start-up, you have little track record nor cash flow (hence you need the loan), and therefore banks shun you. The irony is that banks don't really support you if you need money, but once you have it, they come knocking on your door.

We did secure one business loan during our start-up phase, and it was because Joop put his house up as a personal guarantee. But once that fund was depleted, there was no further opportunity to loan more. (Most entrepreneurs do not have multiple houses to put up for collateral, nor did Joop…)

Venture Capital Firms

The third group we explored were venture capital companies, also known as "VCs," and we approached dozens of them because the start-up scene in Singapore was hip, hot, and happening. I pitched to anyone, from small two-man shops to large prestigious firms, but the responses were almost always disappointing:

"I do not see the '100 X.'"

"It is not risky enough."

"Where is the app?"

"We only invest when we can see the brand in the streets."

"What if 'Green Wireless' comes along?"

Our proposition simply didn't resonate with VCs no matter how much time we spent crafting our "pitch deck."

Everyone who has gone through this process will tell you it is excruciating to go through rejection over and over again, but in hindsight it was a good learning experience. The rejection makes you miserable or angry in the short term (why doesn't anyone understand me?), but over time it makes you mentally stronger, and it made our proposition slightly better every time we had to explain the story. Each time we presented, we got confronted with flaws in our positioning, projections, or plans.

So, if you want to make your business plans better, talk to as many professional investors as you can. They will challenge and ask the difficult questions, which is exactly what you need during your early days of your start-up venture.

During the process, it taught us quite a bit about the VC industry, which is interesting to see. Simply put, VCs are playing the numbers and gambling on securing select high-value wins, similar to placing bets on a single number on a roulette table—except they place dozens of bids across multiple tables. But do not get suckered by the glamour of the fancy VC world; if there is no money for you or if it doesn't come with the right conditions, move on and move quickly. In hindsight, we probably spent too much time on this segment, as eventually not a single VC invested in Blue Wireless. So, what was left?

Angels & Friends

For us, our friends and extended group of acquaintances who always kept asking, "What's Blue Wireless about? What the hell are you guys doing??" became our greatest source of funding throughout our journey.

Over the full span of Blue Wireless, over two dozen angel investors invested in our success, and it became a group that encouraged, supported, and invested in us, many of them at multiple stages.

After the exit, many admitted that after several years they still did not fully understand the specific service the company provided. But they trusted us and the team that we assembled, showing again how important people and personal connections are in your business journey.

Now, of course, taking money from friends is risky (same as employing friends, as I will show later)—and I am sure there are many who recommend against it—but for Blue Wireless, it has been an essential part of the company's success, and without our angel investors, we would not have succeeded in our mission.

Our first investor meeting with (from left to right) Pinaki, Joop, Chin Tat, Ivan, Deepti, Louis, Carsten, Syam, Chris Arscott, Sean, Zac, and two of Pinaki's associates, Singapore, December 2017.

So, if you are considering raising money from friends and family, here are some things we have learned:

First, be open and honest about what you do. Unlike banks and VCs, where you do more of a "dog and pony show" and try to keep the impressions up, you can be much more real and direct with angels, and that is a great plus. Yes, be professional, but give no time for BS, and there is no need to.

Second, share the excitement. Angels, of course, want a return on their investment, and they want their money back, but for many being part of something bigger and supporting a person they know is equally important. While they do not have to work hard and risk all like the founder does, they enjoy being part of the journey. Our WhatsApp group for investors was full of successes, challenges, photos, memes, and more, and people loved being part of it.

Third, only take money if you believe your angels can miss it, and actively ask that question. This is a tough one as you cannot know their exact personal finance situation, but you do not want stressed or overzealous investors breathing down your neck daily because they have their own personal financial issues. This relates also to managing their time and payout expectations as, already mentioned before, building a business will take longer and cost more than projected. In our case, we told early investors a three-to-five-year timeline, which in hindsight was still tight as we managed to exit exactly five years after our first external investment. We communicated clearly up front that there would be no dividend and no payback in the meantime, and there would be further dilutions as we likely needed to raise more. The fundraising did become almost a yearly event, so be ready to ask for money, again and again... It is part of the daily grind, but more about that later.

* * *

As already shown in the best practices above, having many angel investors (instead of one or two big banks/VCs) takes ongoing active management, which means spending time, money, attention, and paperwork on keeping it all going.

Until the exit, I had never engaged a lawyer since I created and executed shareholder agreements, statements, resolutions, and more from common templates on the internet and familiarized myself with the practices and details. While there is some legal risk, managing documents yourself means you can move fast, be flexible, and fully understand all the details of the various arrangements you make, which worked well in the case of Blue Wireless.

While we had some shareholders that exited early by selling their shares to the other shareholders, we never ran into any major issues with this arrangement, and when the exit process started, the shareholders were supportive and patient.

The agreements also outlined the responsibilities of the board, what could be decided by Joop and myself as management, and how shares would be bought and sold. While Joop and I had the majority of shares, we had a single class of shares and thus every investor had the same rights, providing that simplicity and transparency needed for a large group of angel investors.

The board of directors was defined as five positions: two places for Joop and me and three to allow the largest of the angel investors to get more engaged and keep a closer eye on our progress via a board seat. Our board composition remained stable throughout the whole journey with one change when one of the earlier shareholders exited. We met on a call usually every three to six months and tried physically to get together once a year. A good thing was that they came from different backgrounds—one from a finance/private equity background and two with operational experience—so they could give different perspectives. Throughout the journey, I felt that although the board members by themselves did not teach us much that was new about the business itself, their presence and questions and the formality of having to report to them regularly was a good thing. With a board formed from slight "outsider" perspectives, it forces you as an entrepreneur to make sure numbers line up, really think through and document strategic decisions, and answer the hard questions. Also, taking into account their outside perspective is hard but necessary when you are so close to the business on a daily basis.

So, the recommendation is to have a board that is close enough to the business to care (and they really did as they were friends and personally invested) but not too involved in the business or gets involved in operational decisions— ideally they are a team to keep you sharp and on track for your long-term goals.

2.5 THE EARLY SUPPORTERS

The last group belongs to the catchall phrase of "early supporters," all contributing a little bit to your success—whether for stability, promotion, or perspective.

If you're married, it goes without saying that it is essential to get your spouse (and your children if they are old enough) fully on board. Luckily, during the first ten years of my marriage, I had built up enough trust and "credit" that my wife was fully supportive and—after the initial shock had worn off—backed me along the way. Joop was in a similar situation with a stable marriage and stable home.

And as the business progressed, I did keep my wife fully engaged about our developments, strategic decisions, and successes, but I was also careful not to bring problems and frustrations home. It's the same as in a regular job: Leave your issues at the office, otherwise, no part of your personal life is personal anymore. And the same with regular career planning: Your plan of building and exiting your business also needs to align with major events in your personal life, especially children. I was able to keep minimal impact on my children's school schedules and other major parts of our family life (besides working hours), so having my family was a major stability factor.

Again, there are different perspectives on this among entrepreneurs. Some argue that it's best to be single, so you can fully dedicate time and attention to the business, there is nobody to put "at risk" with your crazy adventure, and you have "less mouths to feed." But I saw it differently. Coming home and working for my family gave me enormous purpose and support, because I knew I was not just doing it for myself.

The second group of supporters will emerge from your first customers and early suppliers, and to nurture these relationships is essential. Early business contacts are, of course, important for your business, but some of those will become advisors or even long-term friends. As an entrepreneur, you are passionate about what you do and sincere in your engagements, and you will find that this resonates with many so they will genuinely want to help you. Enthusiasm is contagious, and many that work in larger companies love the passion that entrepreneurs bring—something they often sorely miss in their own jobs or organization. We have had many cases of procurement or product managers in our customers' organizations who knew our product features inside out and became experts in their organization on Blue Wireless services. These ambassadors are essential, and if you come across them, cultivate them. It also gives you confidence that you are on the right track; you need the moral support.

The third group of supporters were several "mentors" who emerged throughout the process, even though technically they would not call themselves that. As I reached out to other entrepreneurs, old managers, and other potential investors for advice (and money), several chats became regular conversations. I listened with care and awe as a Dutch entrepreneur who went through the whole exit process told me about his sleepless nights when he had to make the decision to sell or not, something I would remember later in my journey as well.

Respect those that do not invest money, and do not take rejections personally, as there are many reasons why people do or do not invest.

2.6 THE OTHERS

Well, let me turn it around—who to expect little from?

First, the professionals—the lawyers, accountants, bankers, advisors, and the like. Yes, you might need their help at some point in your journey, but I would not classify them automatically as supporters; they are there for their own paycheck. They are not responsible for your success and do not make the decisions. (And if they do start to get involved in running the business, it is probably because you are in trouble.)

Throughout the journey, we developed a healthy disdain for banks and bankers, especially as they often were more of a hurdle to business success than an enabler. And yes, it is true, once you do have money, they are your friend and will offer you more money. But if you are in need of money or simply services to run your business, their support is nowhere to be seen…

When it came it lawyers, we were maybe a bit extreme because we did not engage a single lawyer in the first seven years of the business. Only when it came to the exit process did we finally engage an outside lawyer to draft materials and represent us in the process.

For the accountants and auditors, we tried to keep the transaction specific to the work that needed to be done.

They are of course useful, but my recommendation is to keep it specific and learn from them but do not let them run your business. They are very good at telling you what you are doing wrong, identifying risks, and coming up with policies and procedures. But in the end, it is your decision on what to do with it. Our financial audit report in the early years had dozens of improvement points that we knew we could not all solve, and in the end, there were many things we consciously decided not to solve or pushed forward to the years ahead. Remember, it is your business and you decide what you spend your time on—having a perfect audit report but being bankrupt is useless…

Lastly, those left behind in your journey can be a source of envy and potentially sabotage. We luckily did not experience it in Blue Wireless, but after speaking to other entrepreneurs, we learned that this is an area to be careful of. It can be ex-colleagues who hold a grudge, ex-investors who did not get what they wanted, or early staff from when things went sour. We were lucky—little drama here.

Key Learnings

- A good cofounder is worth their weight in gold. If you can find someone truly compatible, treat it as a marriage—all in financially and with full transparency.
- Your ownership will dilute over time. Get used to it and learn to trade equity for speed, talent, and survival.
- Angel investors are often more valuable than VCs: They back you as a person first, then your idea.
- Manage your board composition deliberately: close enough to care but not so close that they try to run the business.
- Do not mistake professionals (like lawyers, banks, and auditors) for supporters. They are tools, not your safety net.

3 SURVIVING THE GRIND

From willpower into habit.

3.1 What is the Grind?

So, what is "the grind"? It is the mentality to always keep going, even when things are hard, and never giving up. It is being able to work late at night, early in the morning, and on Saturdays and Sundays. It is the ability to stay positive when you are sometimes not sure if you should keep going or if you are making the right decisions. It is being able to do dull work because no one else is around to do it. It is being able to deal with problems every single day, and after ten years, problem-solving is the daily routine.

The various "grinds": explained in this chapter are those parts of the business that are the essential building blocks that you need to master: sales, marketing, people, money, and service. Sounds like basic business school 101, right?

I thought I was well prepared for starting a business from scratch, as I had both a business degree (economics to be more precise) and experience as a sales manager, a business manager, and finally as a managing director. How difficult could it be?

One thing I forgot is that in all these roles I arrived in a business environment that already was up and running, benefiting from the structures, processes, and systems that people before me had established.

In a start-up environment, it is a different situation. There is nothing at the start, and as such you must create each of these elements from scratch, which requires constant decision-making about how to do things for the first time, without any other person or department to help you. A huge learning curve awaits you.

Wearing multiple hats and doing everything, Singapore, 2017

Secondly, you must be good at all things at the same time. A great engineer but no idea about sales? You are likely to fail. A great salesperson, but no idea about finances? High chance you will run out of money. Even if you are good at two or three core disciplines, "You do not know what you do not know," and that is the start-up predicament.

So, to survive this "grind" of challenges, problems, and unknowns requires more than just information or knowledge. It requires a constant learning attitude, a positive mindset, and just sheer hours to get it right.

Working all the time, everywhere, Singapore 2019

In the coming chapters, I'll dive deeper into the various areas with anecdotes and examples of how we overcame the new challenges when the odds were against us. Each chapter's title starts with "always be" as a reference to the famous line "Always be closing" from Alec Baldwin in the movie *Glengarry Glen Ross*.

3.2 Always be Closing

There are tons of books written about sales techniques and processes and quite a few movies about the art of sales and the struggle of being a salesperson. Anyone who has been in the sales profession would know titles like *Wall Street* or *Boiler Room*, but the most legendary in my opinion is called *Glengarry Glen Ross*, about a team of real estate salespeople trying to get through their day and close deals.

The movie has a famous monologue of fifteen minutes from a brilliant, but offensive, sales manager played by Alec Baldwin. As he tried to motivate his team and explained the principles of sales, he kept repeating "*A-B-C*—always be closing," one of the key factors in being successful in sales.

The other famous line from his speech is "Put that coffee down, coffee is for closers only"—a printout of which has hung above our Nespresso machine since the start of our business and was moved to each new office we expanded to.

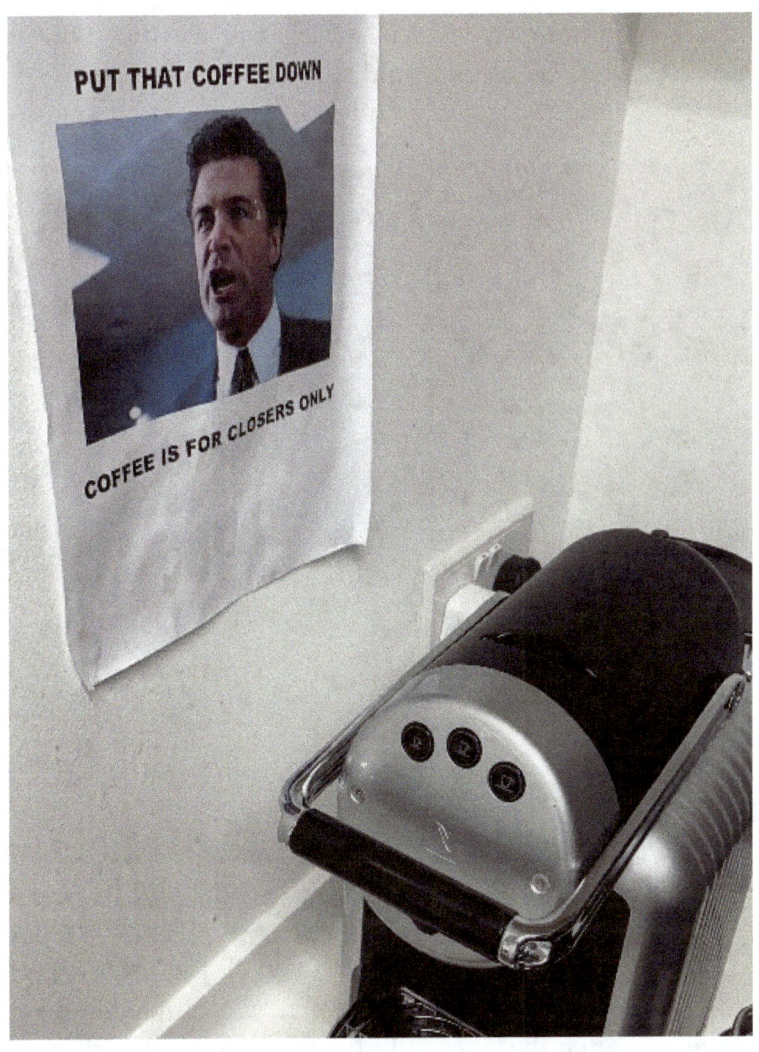

Coffee machine at the Blue Wireless office, Singapore, 2018

"Always be closing" in a startup environment means several things:

First, always be explaining. In Blue Wireless, we offered a new, innovative service and, as most new start-ups do, we had to continuously explain what it is we did, how it worked, what the value would be, etc.

Joop explaining again at a start-up event, Singapore, 2016

And even for customers who we met multiple times, it appeared often that they still did not fully grasp it. So, we explained it again and again and again, and so should you. Never assume the sale is done or the deal or order is in the bag: Always be showing the value, explaining, and closing.

Second, everyone sells. There is no sales department. As a founder you must become the best salesperson possible, and you can be since you are now the only person to have detailed insight into the specifics of the product or service. Also, with every interaction, you get feedback and insight into what customers like or dislike, which things work, or which aspects need improvement. That accumulation of knowledge is extremely powerful and the more sales interactions you have, the better you get. But it cannot be a one-man show; everyone in the company who interacts with customers, but also with suppliers or anyone in the industry, needs to know the company pitch and be able to explain your proposition and interest—and ideally close—a customer.

Third, always be qualifying—qualification is the hardest job for a salesperson, as we tend to be overly optimistic and expect positive outcomes from each inquiry or sales interaction. Not every customer is the right one, and bad customers can slow you down in growing your business or, worst case, bring you to the brink of bankruptcy.

But qualification criteria change over time. In the early phase, you are very much focused on just making a sale, getting traction, and especially generating some cash. And a customer who offers you a check in hand (yes, those still exist in Singapore and other countries) increases their own closure success rate to 100 percent and are the ones to act upon immediately. This is even more if customers are willing to pay up front, up to the point where a customer becomes a de facto financier of your business.

In Blue Wireless, we had this situation with one customer in Australia who, through a trusted relationship and extremely proactive and skillful work from Joop, was willing to pay one year in advance. It was unique for us at time when the majority of customers then paid thirty to sixty days in arrears. The flipside of the deal was that they expected—rightfully so—serious commitment in time and resource from Joop personally, slowing down the progress and growth we were trying to achieve in other segments of the business. But in hindsight, it was the right decision and anyone who offers cash in the early phase of your start-up should be welcomed with open arms, as you need to stay afloat to be able to work further on building the business.

Then, there are those opportunities that allow you to take your business to the next level. These are critical—keep your eyes wide open for them as you need them to scale. Sir Richard Branson is quoted as saying, "If somebody offers you an amazing opportunity but you are not sure you can do it, say yes—then learn how to do it later." Some customers give you an opportunity to expand in new areas or stretch yourself to a new level, even if they are less profitable or if it requires you to deliver something that you do not have readily available yet. But if that allows you to further your strategic objectives, go for it and you will see yourself rise to the challenge.

In Blue Wireless, we had several moments where we had to extend ourselves to make the impossible possible, including a project in early 2018 for luxury retailer Coach. In their contract with AT&T they required wireless connectivity for over four hundred stores across Asia, with the majority in Japan. Until that time, we had delivered only a handful of locations in Japan, limited actual experience, and one single contractor who spoke Japanese. How could we implement connectivity for four hundred stores? We took a calculated gamble, and as the project started to get traction, we saw new ideas coming and people taking initiative, allowing us to pull it off. These were ideas and initiatives that probably would not have appeared if we weren't forced to deliver. Six years later, the services are still running, and Coach remains one of our key customers in the Asia Pacific region.

The girls from the Singapore team during Christmas 2018—who I promised Coach wallets if we landed the deal, and we did!

Lastly, as you get more traction and generate more consistent cash flow, it is essential that you focus on those opportunities that will bring long-term revenue—as those will be the ones that your future acquirer will be paying for. Those customers need to be long-term, profitable, and sustainable, which probably means that you need to update your criteria again, away from short-term deals and away from risky bets, but find customers which match your long-term outlook.

So, in conclusion, the qualification of customer opportunities is key: initially those who bring cash, then those who allow you to stretch and scale, and then those who are the right fit for the long-term exit.

3.3 Always be Promoting

No matter how big or small your idea or how simple or ambitious your venture is, you need to market it and for that you need a brand. Branding is not just for the consumer brands you see in the supermarket or the ads and billboards. A clear brand is essential for any business, especially when starting up. It is fundamental for creating interest with customers, closing and keeping them, and attracting staff, investors, and vendors. But it's also essential for yourself: You are building a dream; you need to be able to make that dream visual and tangible.

One of my marketing mentors told me that the basic premise of marketing is "focus and repetition," and if you look at the largest brands today in the world, you will see this pattern confirmed. Have a singular message and keep on repeating that at each and every turn in the physical and online world until you, your customers, and your staff are literally sick and tired of it.

Personally, I have always loved marketing as a discipline, and for a business-to-business venture, probably spent a larger proportion than average of my time on it since as I enjoyed the work and have been told I'm good at it. It almost became my escape work. If I needed a break from more boring work, I always found the energy to get back to making leaflets, presentations, and LinkedIn posts.

For Blue Wireless, the branding journey started with the name, which came quickly after the previous steps of defining my dream and ideal product-market combination. After knowing that I wanted to address global corporate customers with a new Internet access option, the search for a suitable name started. I began researching corporate brands and branding in general, and I was inspired by the simplicity of the major brands with generic names, such as Apple, which have little in common with the product itself but are short and sweet. Within the telco industry, there were more like these, Orange for instance. Companies like Orange or Virgin combined their brands with products, such as Orange Business or Virgin Mobile—simple, clean, and easy to expand upon when needed. And we were starting in the new segment of wireless networking that is different from mobile, which is all about phones and consumers.

That simple childhood question of what your favorite color is has, for me, always been easy to answer—blue! Yes, most of my clothing is blue, the cars I drove were blue, and while hard to explain, the blue color just gives me a feeling that fits my character. But to further analyze the color used in brands, blue stands for stability, integrity, and reliability, which was fitting for our audience of corporates who are more conservative compared to other segments, such as consumers, small business, residential, etc. As an additional bonus, blue is associated with the sky, openness, and new opportunity, which was ideal for a new business specializing in wireless communications that run through the skies to connect customers, rather than the traditional wired lines that rely on underground cabling.

Combining "blue" and "wireless" into "Blue Wireless" was an easy step from there. I did have a few alternatives, such as "Blue Link" and some others, which I'm too embarrassed to share. After repeating it in my head for a few days, I was ready for the next step—the logo.

Nike's logo was famously designed by an intern, and she was paid seventeen US dollars for the work (and many shares later when Nike went to an initial public offering), but probably both the designer and Phil Knight, the Nike cofounder, never knew how iconic and impactful it would be over time.

So, I wanted to spend some good time and effort on getting it right. Logo design today has been largely taken over by AI, but in 2015 it was done by auction type websites where different designers submitted their proposals based on a brief, and the winner gets paid. I created a brief that explained our purpose of offering something unique (wireless) to a global market (corporates) and the "feeling" that I wanted to convey. The latter was a hard one as I wanted to balance between the ideas of wireless and innovation without being "techie" while still giving comfort and showing reliability. And of course, the color I had already. For a mere 200 Singapore dollars the logo design competition started and I was overwhelmed with dozens of different designs. The great thing about wading through all these designs was that I could define what I did *not* want, which is half the battle. Eventually, I selected an Australian designer, and she and I fine-tuned it until it was to my liking, showing something representing a stable "core" or SIM card, with a wave representing the wireless connectivity through the air. The logo was born!

Getting your logo and name right from the start is crucial, and I strongly suggest reading up on this as there is quite some literature on it, so I will not go into the mechanics. But having gone through the process itself, I did see a few common mistakes in the early start-up scene in 2015:

- First, overly "techie" or difficult names, replacing letters with numbers, replacing the *s* with a *z* and so forth ("networkz4u"). While it may be great for the engineers who work there, it's unlikely to resonate with customers, whether consumers or businesses.
- Second, trying to say too much. One or two words is the maximum. And those logos that have slogans within the design quickly get way too crowded.
- Third, being too small/local. "Shiok Meats" is a cool twist for those living in Singapore and know what the local slang word is, but if your ambition is to go big, think about the future—would people outside of Singapore understand it? Does it scale?

Normally, the next step in brand design after defining a name and a logo is to create a slogan. Many times, I have been asked what it was for Blue Wireless. Simple answer: We did not have one. At least not just one. Over the years, there have been different messages and slogans, and we adjusted it as our company evolved and to whom we communicated.

The first Blue Wireless banner with our first slogan, Singapore, 2016

Three slogans or taglines stood out over time:

1. **"Access Anywhere."** I created this day one, emphasizing the key premise of our service: It works anywhere. And "access" was short for "local access," which is a well-understood term in the networking industry.
2. **"Enabling the Wireless Enterprise."** We started using this around 2018 inspired by Cradlepoint, the need for more complex solutions, and the attempt to be more visionary, not a one-trick pony, but more-solutions based. I had the feeling, however, that it did not always resonate with people, since many probably wondered: What is a "wireless enterprise"?

3. **"Worry-Free Wireless."** This started around 2021 when we refreshed more of our branding and reimagined what made us special as Blue Wireless, emphasizing our people- and service-first approach.

A slogan can be very important depending on your market proposition, but for our service, which was more complex and evolving, it was more important that we were very clear and consistent in the wording and terms used in our communication. Ideally, your target is to "own" one or more of the specific words that continuously are repeated to explain and differentiate yourself. For Blue Wireless, there were a few:

Firstly: "wireless." This might seem obvious, since it is in our company name, but in the telecommunication industry in 2015, the main word used for our type of services was "mobile," referring to "mobile networks." Many of our later competitors continued to use the word "mobile," which I believe put them at a disadvantage, as it has this strong connection to mobile phones, the consumer market, etc. In none of our communications since our start did we ever used the word "mobile." Yes, we use mobile networks and mobile technologies, but ours is not "mobile"; it is "wireless." It is different. It is newer. It is better.

Second word: "global". It was a bold statement for a small company, but it reflected our ambition and our key target group of multinational companies. We always peppered the word "global" into our communications, again, trying to elevate ourselves to where we needed to be, not where we were at the time.

Third word: "service." We were always providing a service, a capability; we "enabled" something. While competitors were selling routers, SIM cards, and antennas, we were selling a service. Now, this did not make it easier, because services are intangible and much harder to market, but it provided the necessary differentiation from others. Also, we lost a lot of business since many companies were in the market to buy components, not the service, but more about that later...

3.4 Always Be Evolving Your Brand

So, with the logo, name, color, and words in hand, what's next? Market research, focus groups, marketing communication plans, advertising budget? No, just start, simple, close to home, and keep expanding and repeating from there. "Guerilla marketing" is the way to go here. If you do not know what it is, read up on it, as you will have to start punching way above your weight, making more impact with less time, money, and people and no reputation.

In the case of Blue Wireless, as a new entrant in the corporate telecommunication market, the company was a nobody on day one; it was literally me working out of my guest bedroom. How to convince prospects and customers you can do it?

Solution: Start building on your own reputation (network!) by borrowing your reputation from cofounders or early staff and the work they have accomplished in previous jobs. In the case of Blue Wireless, Joop and I had a combined fifty years' worth of telco experience in the industry, so that gave us a good foundation. (Again, this is a reason why you shouldn't start a business in a completely new industry.)

One of the many, many, many presentations given...

Besides leveraging your past reputation, the next step is giving samples, free products/services, or in our case of a service a "proof of concept", which is a way to demonstrate your service. Any opportunity you have to deliver your product or service—whether customers pay a lot or little or nothing—take it! This will give you the opportunity to demonstrate but more importantly to learn and build your reputation.

In the early days of Blue Wireless, we went out on a limb to get the service up and running, saying yes to the craziest requests and flying to different countries to install, get traction, and get the first customers interested. Even if the customers did not pay or continue, it helped build up our reputation since at the next customer inquiry we were able to name-drop the previous customer and location. We actually delivered one service to a mine in Mongolia, and, oh my, we used that example for years! Early customers want proof and seeing is believing, especially for a service or product that is not proven, so keep taking photos wherever you can.

Once we had the bits and pieces of actual services going, we had to get the word out, and we used four main pillars for our marketing communications: our newsletter, socials, website, and events.

Wireless Wednesday

I came up with the name "Wireless Wednesday" in late 2015, and it became the regular weekly newsletter for Blue Wireless. I sent the first edition to approximately two hundred of my contacts, friends, and family in October of that year. I tried to educate readers about what wireless internet was about, the differences between technologies, practical tips, and, of course, our services and our progress as a company. Over the coming years, no matter whose email address I was able to get my hands on, they were added to the database and received my emails for years to come. My friends surely noticed the barrage of weekly emails and pulled a nice prank on me during one of our boys trips. When main course was served and everyone received steaks on their plate, the waiter ceremoniously brought out a plate with a can of Spam on it!

For the first five years of Blue Wireless, I would write a Wireless Wednesday almost every single week and kept adding people and business cards. It took me at least one hour every week, but I enjoyed doing it, and it became a well-read communication, as we could see from the newsletter statistics who would open what message.

It was in 2022 when we had close to ten thousand subscribers, and we finally reduced the frequency from weekly to once a month—after which my mother actually asked, "Hey, I did not get your newsletter last week, what happened?" Clearly someone was reading it!

Ten years on, with so much content out there produced daily, newsletters lost a little bit of their impact, but during the early days of Blue Wireless, it was a firm pillar in getting the word out.

Getting Social

LinkedIn was the second marketing pillar and a major contributor to the success of Blue Wireless, allowing us to reach the global, professional audience that we wanted to connect to.

When you are a new entrant in the market, building up an online presence is not easy, but you have to start acting like you have been around forever and you deserve a seat at the table.

So, full disclosure, I bought my first Blue Wireless LinkedIn followers from a freelancer online for fifty US dollars. And amazingly, few days later, we had over five hundred followers, giving instant credibility. Greatest ROI (return on investment) ever.

But the same as with the newsletter, building up a base of followers took time. And after that first five hundred though, it was really one at a time, and I built personal followers and company followers simultaneously.

With any new connection I made in real life, I always connected with them online diligently, and I actively searched daily on LinkedIn for more contacts in our industry and potential customer audience. My title back then was not "CEO" but my self-styled "Chief Wireless Officer." It often got a chuckle from the people who read what was on my business card, and it was a great conversation starter.

I also made sure that there was continuous content on both personal and company pages, whether it was sharing serious business insights, service installs we completed, photos from the latest travels, and even changing the Blue Wireless logo color for Dutch King's Day (orange) and the day Prince died (purple).

And over time, as I continued to connect, publish, share, and connect some more, momentum started to happen. People started to notice what we were doing, credibility started to grow, and potential customers and candidates started to reach out. By the end of 2025, we reached over twenty-five thousand real followers on our company page, and it has become an essential part of our identity as a business.

Our Website

I was able to register the domain bluewireless.asia, which was a bit unconventional, but still a great match at the start of Blue Wireless due to our Asia Pacific focus.

Obviously, I wanted the bluewireless.com domain for a more global corporate appeal, but it was owned by a small, local US carrier in New York state called..."Blue Wireless." That Blue Wireless offered local mobile plans to consumers but mostly used the domain name blueunlimited.com.

In 2018, I noticed that their domain bluewireless.com was actually for sale through a broker, and I enquired. The asking price was 10,000 US dollars, which at that stage of our journey was a huge amount for something nonbusiness critical. But after several weeks of back-and-forth, I pulled the trigger and acquired the domain, which was an important building block in our ambitious plan to go global.

The US company "Blue Wireless" continued for a little longer and eventually folded in 2020.

In our segment, there were several other "blue" companies that led to confusion at some stage—to name a few: Ice Blue, Blu Wireless, Blues Wireless, FastBlue, Blue Ocean Wireless. None were direct competitors, and we outgrew them all...

Some confusion about the name Blue Wireless in the US, 2020

On the Road

Some of the best networking was done during events, which we attended wherever we could. There was a lot of hit-and-miss in those early days, as we attended anything from "start-up events" to "5G events," but we kept telling our story over and over again, slightly adjusting and improving each time.

By 2019, we approached a more serious level since we had stands at CommunicAsia and other industry events, and we leveraged our early technology partner Cradlepoint wherever we could.

Brand overload at the CommunicAsia event, Singapore, 2019

The combination of social media, events, recurring newsletters, and the personal touch created ever more momentum and marketing work, and it was time to hire my first marketing support staff.

During the first three-and-a-half years, I ran all marketing activities myself, from LinkedIn to the newsletters to our website to events to mousepads. Since I had direct contact with customers every day, deciding on activities and messages was quick and efficient, unlike having to explain it to outsourced marketing agencies who then overcomplicate it, slow you down, and require additional funds.

In any case, when creating any content, ads, copy, or visuals, do not sweat it and go with your gut. Yes, basic quality checks are needed (the right blue in our case), but especially on social media, the average lifespan is a few hours, two days at best. "So what" if an ad or post is a bit quirky or off, the world turns fast. While large organizations need to be extremely careful regarding their reputation and compliance, as a start-up, you can afford some glitches here and there, as long as you keep communicating 24/7.

In the beginning, agility, speed, and flexibility are your main differentiators against your competitors who are all bigger. Use that flexibility, for instance, in how you do your marketing campaigns. While your budget is small, you can create a campaign in a day, while incumbents often need committees and many weeks to get approvals.

For example, there were strings of internet fiber outages that occurred in Singapore in 2017 that made the news. Within a few hours, we started posting on social media the benefits of wireless internet (no fiber cuts) and then extended that to Google Ads to show how wireless internet offers an alternative.

Early on, I also had extra email addresses, even for fictional people, to look like a bigger company. One email address I created during my first year was for Jack, our PR manager. Obviously, there was no such person, but when sending out the first press releases and newsletters, I wanted to look bigger and have some more names on there than just myself: so, "In case of media enquiries, please contact jack@bluewireless.asia." I thought the name was fitting given I was a jack-of-all-trades, but it worked. A funny thing happened several years later when I got a spam call from a call center and someone was asking for Jack from PR!

If you adopt the guerilla marketing mindset, it is surprising what you can get away with and achieve without conforming to the assumed norms. Ask for forgiveness, not for permission.

While ad hoc marketing is the start, you cannot keep up the approach forever, and eventually you will need to build a process around it, hire people who see the vision, and further develop it. Like anything in your business, your brand needs to evolve, and for Blue Wireless, this came around year five, 2020, when we had built up the business to a substantial level enough to know that we were on a good trajectory.

Looking back at the previous years, we had accomplished so much at that moment in figuring out our customers, technology, finances, and more. My new marketing manager in the Netherlands helped me do some soul-searching about what made us really unique. At the end of several interesting brainstorming sessions, we came to an interesting conclusion: We were not unique because of the fact that LTE/5G was faster and cheaper, nor our global reach, or all the other good selling points that we always emphasized in our communications. We were (and are) unique because of our people.

In a previous company I worked at in the '90s (Infonet), the slogan was "A Network of Technology and People" and five years into Blue Wireless, that was exactly what we had become: a group of fifty around the world working as a global team to serve our customers.

As our marketing manager started to redesign our wording and imagery used on the websites, the hard part for any founder comes: letting go. You realize it is not your brand anymore; it is not your company—it has a life of its own, supported by people internally and recognized by people externally. It continuously evolves as the company and the people in it have daily interactions and communications. Yes, you can steer it and guide it, but you cannot fully control it anymore and you shouldn't.

Like everything in the business that evolves, this is one that needs to evolve as well. And depending on your stage and your success, it might need a reset or pivot or overhaul. Whatever it is, keep evolving and do not get stuck in the past, as the assumptions of the beginning are not valid anymore.

3.5 ALWAYS BE HIRING

In most business models, once your volume of customers, orders, and revenues grow, your workload is likely to grow as well and besides automation (more on that later), people are the essential building block in supporting this growth.

Having the right number of people for the amount of work is tricky, and you will probably be overstaffed or understaffed at various points in your journey. At Blue Wireless, we have been in both situations.

Manju handling incoming shipments, Singapore, 2018

Having too few people means the work quality will suffer, which will impact customers, but more importantly, it will put long hours and stress on your staff and yourself, which you can only tolerate for so long. Continuously being understaffed is unsustainable, and staff will eventually quit, leaving you with an ever-bigger problem than before. Understaffing will also hamper your ability to try new things and work on improvements and will slow your long-term growth progress.

Having too many people for the current workload sounds like an expensive waste, but that is where you ideally need to aim for, as the reality is that if you don't keep growing, you will never get there.

Let me explain:

First, of all the "cycles" in your business, the people aspect has one of the longest business cycles from start to finish, and I dare say it will take at least six to twelve months from initial interest to productive employee. So, you need to recruit in advance for the company you will want to have in the future.

Second, people will quit at some point, and you do not always control this. Of course, it is essential that you have some career planning options and look out for development opportunities. But the reality is that in a small start-up company the options to move to a different role or become a manager are small. And, in many cases, you will be paying less than standard in a market with larger firms who have more resources. So, a significant number of staff will quit at some point, you just do not know when. We had some cases in Blue Wireless where, in a period of four months, three sales staff quit, not because of unhappiness, but because their time was "up." When this happened, it left a serious dent in our ability to execute for months, while we frantically recruited new team members.

Lastly, your needs will evolve over time, and some people are not suitable since they will struggle to adapt to the ever-changing needs of the company. So, you will need to let some people go at some point. Besides the actual process of firing people, the timing of when to let people go is also tricky. In hindsight, in Blue Wireless, we often kept people around for too long after they were no longer performing or not suitable for the needs of the company. Here, the loyalty towards those who supported you in the beginning or fear of interrupting any operations plays a role, but in the cases where we finally pulled the trigger and let people go, things worked out quickly. So, some advice: Fire quickly.

But since you are in a growing organization, staff will leave and some staff need to be let go at some point. You are in constant need of new people, and thus recruitment needs to be an essential part of your business operations.

Over the years, Joop and I have literally done hundreds of interviews each and developed a key skill every entrepreneur needs to develop: how to read people. It is not an easy one and certainly not one that I can claim to be fully proficient in, but here are some tips:

- **Hire for attitude, train for skills.** The mantra remains, whether in the very early days or scaling up. Without the right motivation or attitude, it is difficult for staff to thrive, especially in a start-up environment. Skills can be learned, people with a wrong attitude (entitled, afraid, lazy, you name it) will not succeed.
- **In case of doubt, do not.** Especially when we had multiple interviews with different staff, if one person had doubts, we passed on the candidate and let him or her go. Many times, I was the one who wanted to hire, believing that candidates would rise to the challenge or feeling the pressure from the business to hire quickly, and luckily a second interviewer expressed his or her doubts, and we did not proceed.
- **Be aware of your biases, but do not try to eliminate them all.** You are not working for a large

corporation or government where hiring is under strict supervision and an almost anonymous affair. If you are hiring for a start-up, you will be working much more closely and likely under more pressure than an average established company, so it is OK to hire people who match your personal interests or with whom you can get along. Hire people you like!
- **Look for growth potential.** Does this person have the potential to become a manager who can lead a portion of the business or a team? It's difficult to assess during initial interviews, but it's something that will be very valuable for the future since you need managers in the company as you grow. And you should really try to promote from within rather than trying to hire managers halfway through your journey who will lead the early joiners.

Just note that in most cases, you will be in a scarce job market where you are competing for talent. It is very much a two-way selection, and thus positioning the company, yourself, and the vision is essential to compete with other companies out there.

3.6 Always be Serving

Besides managing sales, marketing, and people, the actual service is what customers want and why you are in business. And it is the only thing which is always on, 24/7. While the other things can take a break, service cannot, at least not if you are trying to build a reputation and want to build long-term revenue from loyal customers.

In most service businesses, the rule is simple. You only start making money over time: returning customers means more orders means recurring revenue—that is where the profit is. Your first engagements usually cost money and more effort than what they bring in, so getting over that initial hump needs your full and undivided attention.

Testing 4G connectivity at the Vopak site, Sebarok, Singapore, 2017

This chapter should be dedicated to Joop and my first hire Syam, since they made so much of this happen in the initial years. They made sure all the pieces came together and the technology worked and kept working. They spent literally thousands of hours—often during weekends and late nights—figuring things out: configuring, testing, deploying, installing, ripping out, fixing, and trying again for literally hundreds of services. The learning curve was steep, like so many parts of the business, but as a founder, it is essential that you know your "product" inside and out, and oh yes, we did.

Joop was relentless in finding solutions to real-life problems. We encountered them in the field as we tried to deploy our first Cradlepoint routers in countries that they were not designed to work in. Often, we gave the engineers at Cradlepoint headquarters insights into the bugs and improvements that were needed. In 2017, only two years in, we surprisingly were awarded Cradlepoint Partner of the Year since likely they never saw two founders so obsessed with making things work as we were.

But it was not just technical; we were constantly figuring things out and slowly building our "global service model." How do we ship noncertified equipment into Vietnam? (Declare them as household goods.) How do we accept Indonesian rupiah in Singapore? (I opened a local account.) How do we get local SIM cards in Thailand? (My wife registered a company.) The list of creative solutions was growing by the day, and there was never a problem we couldn't overcome. Although I'm a terrible engineer (I do not read instructions, nor take directions very well), by installing and configuring the earlier services myself, it became second nature; we could do this in our sleep. Joop and I were constantly coming up with solutions to everything that was thrown to us, and with every problem solved, we became more confident that we could do this.

As Elon Musk once put it: "If you do not genuinely enjoy solving hard problems, you will hate being an entrepreneur—because that is the job description."

The irony of the grind is that the better you become at solving problems, the more problems the world sends your way. That is the tax you pay on success.

Joop with our first 5G installation completed, Sydney, early 2020

As we expanded our capabilities and reach, we promised ever-greater service levels to our customers: seventy-two hours delivery, 24/7 support, 99.9 percent uptime. None of these points were fully possible yet in reality, but it started to position us with the companies we wanted to compete with: IT service providers.

What we did not fully realize at that moment was that problem-solving alone was not sufficient, and our approach was not scalable, but it set the tone of how we were building the business. If you are building a business—this part is nonnegotiable—be obsessed with service. Always on call, always available. Or as we called it "Joop to the rescue"!

3.7 Always Keep Your Eye On The Money

Besides having to manage sales and marketing, hire great people, and deliver excellent service, you will be spending an awful amount of time on managing money—raising it, collecting it, accounting for it, spending it. It is the oil in the machine that makes everything work, and the lack of money is one of your greatest risks to achieving a successful business. Even if your customers like what you do, even if your margin is positive, and even if you might be making a profit on paper, it is about having cash and having it at the right time and right place, which is a full-time job. And even if you have enough to run today's operations, if you want to grow, you need to finance the growth of tomorrow. So be prepared to always look for more money. It is maddening...

Now, the first thing most entrepreneurs think about is that money just comes from investors or customers. But there are many more angles to how you manage this daily, so let's get started:

Making Money

As your number of customers grows, so does the volume of quotes, invoices, and collections. Keeping track of all of it is complex, despite sales teams, finance departments, and automation.

So, the first rule of generating cash is to make sure things are delivered, as without it, you cannot charge. Simple enough right? Well, it may be if you are delivering a physical product where there is a clear handover to the customer, but in the case of services, things tend to drag on: Customers are not ready to receive, something is not quite right, or something could be done better, etc. I've always been pushy on this portion of the business to make sure that service "delivery" is a continuing process, as we can only charge customers once it is up and running. But more about this in the chapter on scaling.

Second, make sure that what is being delivered is actually invoiced. Again, it's a very basic concept but difficult in execution once you have hundreds of service elements across dozens of countries. Even in 2025, every month or so, we came across something where we did the work but somehow forgot to invoice, often for months and a few times for many thousands of dollars.

Then comes the fun part: collections. My learning curve in collections was steep. In one of my previous jobs at BT Global Services, my revenue responsibility was close to 40 million US dollars per year, generated by wholesale customers across the Asia Pacific region. For the big prestigious customer names, shown nicely in our Excel sheets and PowerPoint presentations, I never had to worry about the actual collection of these amounts—and to be frank, I was completely clueless about how this money even reached our company.

The first customer order Blue Wireless ever received was from Mundipharma. It was for the rental of a Wi-Fi router for their new factory opening in Singapore where they were expecting a lot of dignitaries and media, however, they had no Wi-Fi at the location. The first delivery was successful, and a few days later, I received my first check in the mail. Blue Wireless was officially in business!

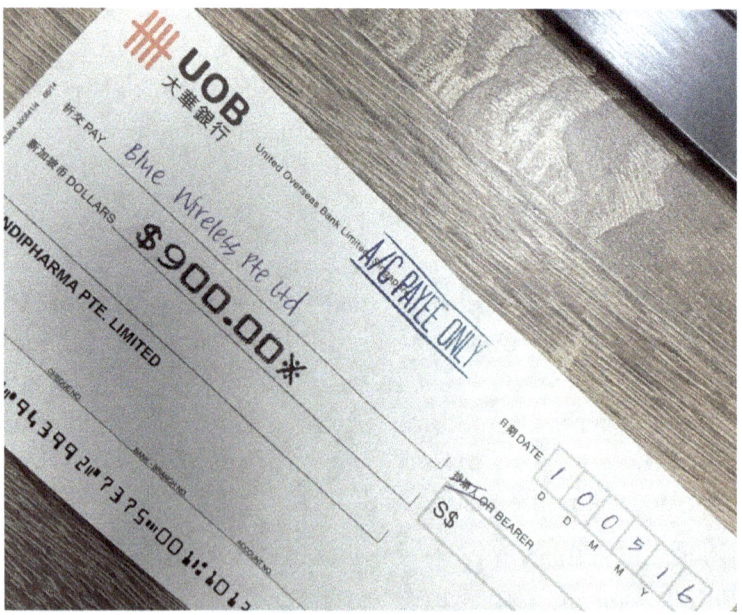

First customer check ever, Singapore, 2016

Fast forward to year three in Blue Wireless and approaching one hundred customers: Several had invoices overdue for months, running into the tens of thousands of dollars, which was impacting not only cash flow but frankly also morale and pride. Why were they not paying? We sent them so many reminders, turned off their services, and pleaded with them. What were we doing wrong? I started Googling "late payments," and of course collection agencies and law firms topped the list, but was that the way to go? The realization set in that no one else was going to help; the buck stopped with me.

Finally, on one Monday afternoon, I had enough, printed out the overdue invoices, and got in the car to personally collect the ones around the industrial estates in Singapore. The first company was not even there anymore at the listed unit; a cleaner gave me the new address details. Arriving at the office and with nobody opening the front door, I found the employees' entrance and walked in, casually asking a staff member in a cubicle where Mr. Tan, their finance manager, was seated. After finding his office, I took a seat on an empty chair, handed over my business card and the printed invoices, and told him I was there to collect payment. He started stumbling about that I should have sent him an email, that everyone was out for lunch, and that his assistant would take care of it. But I did not move and told him I would not leave that chair until I saw the payment in my hand or in the company bank account.

I will not quickly forget the surprise on his face as suddenly people started moving about, and the invoice was "found" in their system. Ten minutes later, I saw the amount in our account. Twenty minutes after that, I was in the car with a massive adrenaline rush, on the way to two more addresses with the same approach. Again, I put myself down and vowed not to leave until I had the money. By the end of the afternoon, I collected 18,000 Singapore dollars. I never felt so triumphant in my life.

No business school or accounting course can prepare you for this. And until you feel the dire need for more money so you can pay yourself or your staff, you will not come out of your comfort zone. When it comes to collecting money from customers, be on top of it like a hawk. Nonpaying customers can break your business easily, and paper guarantees and lawyers are worthless. Keep checking your outstanding collectibles every month, and as you grow, make sure your sales and finance team is on top of those, as it is the best source of money for your business.

Spending Money

Second best source of money? Not spending it or paying for it yet. The "not spending" portion is hard, at least for me. In my personal life, I'm not extravagant or wasteful, but I'm hardly frugal. And same for Joop. We always had and used money to buy quality items or enable us to do the things we wanted to do. Yes, we "bootstrapped" our business: going for the cheaper options, doing things ourselves, delaying purchases, and reducing our comfort to save small amounts—which in hindsight was not really the best use of our time—but there was simply no other choice, and we expected the same from our staff.

IKEA furniture was the default and putting it together ourselves was normal. Painting walls blue, doing our own construction was standard practice. It was so standard that it almost became a badge of honor for the new joiners at new offices if they put together their own desks and chairs. Economy flights and cheap accommodation were normal; I travelled mostly on public transport for years. And during that time, it hardly bothered me at all.

The team putting together IKEA furniture for our new office, Amsterdam, 2022

It is surprising what you can get away with in terms of delaying payment on things. As the saying goes, "All is fair in love and war"—well, it should be updated to start-ups. Remember, you are fighting for survival, so you should delay payments where you can, and many suppliers will let you. But this is a process to manage, not ignore. In Blue Wireless, we always kept a priority list in terms of payment:

1. **Staff**. The payment of salaries are nonnegotiable, although at times you might need to exclude yourself from payment.
2. **Taxes**. Do not skimp on VAT (value-added tax)/GST (goods and services tax) or any other taxes. It will hurt, but getting those out of the way is essential, as the government can be brutal and powerful if you miss these—they will be the first ones to push for bankruptcy.
3. **Critical suppliers**. Always pay those that are essential for your business operations and the delivery of goods and services. For Blue Wireless, this included all SIM data suppliers obviously, so our monthly services could keep running.
4. **Noncritical suppliers**. Push everything else: even rent, or those who already provided products and services. (What can they do? Take them back?) Again, do not ignore them, but communicate and stretch the deadlines—thirty to sixty to ninety days or more beyond the payment date.

When collections are maximized and supplier payments deadlines are stretched, you will likely still need more money, so the third source is raising funds.

Always be Raising

In a venture business, the need for ever more (working) capital continues as you pursue growth and try to build long-term value. Unless you hit the start-up jackpot and you can finance your growth from your free cash flow, you will likely need more cash from outside, which means more money from investors.

It is a devilish dilemma; you need more cash to grow and survive, and for founders, taking more investor money means diluting your share in the company. It hurts your pride and your senses, but it is a mental barrier you need cross to keep going. The best way to deal with it is not just to look at how much this will "cost" you in future payout, but by how much this dilution will increase the value of your business and how much it will increase your chances of making it successful. This is an important concept and calculation to understand. Simply put, the relative increase in share price should be larger than your relative reduction in ownership.

During the initial seven years, we raised money from around twenty people through over forty transactions, but we can break it down into four segments:

- **The initial funding.** This was Joop and I. We set a nominal share price based on what we put in. Calculations were easy.
- **The first round.** Setting an initial price with angel investors was hard. What was it worth? The current value? The potential value? Multiples of revenue or profit did not mean much as we had little to show for it. We set an initial share price and managed to close our first round with eight investors. Joop and I reduced our shareholding significantly. We thought we were safe and well-funded for the future…
- **More rounds followed.** During the roughly four years that followed, we continue to need money

every year. The business grew, but the cash flow dwindled faster. Difficult decisions about whether to expand and raise again usually meant going back to the investors for more. Several new investors joined, and we were able to raise the price of the new shares issued, which meant existing shareholders felt good and new ones saw growth.

- **The final rounds.** Once we made the decision to sell in 2022, we thought the end was in sight and a new buyer would solve all our cash problems. But in the months that it dragged on and on, we needed more cash to keep up the growth and our good performance for potential buyers, which meant again raising more. This time we did get more creative with loans as well as convertible loans, which were less "costly" from an ownership perspective.

While our model of friendly angel investors worked out well, fundraising became one of our many full-time jobs.

Besides raising money for the company, there might be instances where you as a founder must sell shares outright to other investors. Both Joop and I had to do this at some point so we could pay off (some) of our personal obligations and debt, which were also accumulating as time went on.

It was necessary at the time, but this is financially worse than issuing new shares and diluting your ownership for multiple reasons: First, you are selling at the current value rather than keeping your shares and diluting, which means that you keep your shares for future value. Second, the money does not go into the business, so it doesn't help with building and reaching that future value. Sell your shares only in emergency situations, which for us it was, but in hindsight, do not sell and borrow more money if you can. In the end, both Joop and myself diluted our shares through the years until our combined ownership at exit was just 54 percent.

Elon Musk said in the early years of SpaceX that they were always "one launch away from bankruptcy." And while our ambitions (or egos) were not as large as Elon's, it felt like financially we were always living on the edge, ready to fall off a cliff—not just as a company but also personally.

Most months I was what we call in Dutch "filling one hole with another," which the English call "robbing Peter to pay Paul." Similar as the payment priority in the business, I practiced the same at home, and usually I was last, which literally meant four dollars in my account in some of the early years.

Doing all these things continuously ourselves for the initial years—selling, promoting, hiring, delivering, servicing, raising funds, grinding away—I wondered to myself sometimes: How did we survive and not collapse? How did we keep our sanity? More about that in the next chapters.

Key Learnings

- *The grind never ends: You must learn, build, and experience every function of the business yourself before anyone helps you.*
- *Sales never stops. Everyone sells, and you must explain your value a hundred times.*
- *Customer qualification is key: choose the type that matches the stage of the business.*
- *Branding starts simple: Focus + repetition + speed is more important than big budgets. Guerilla marketing lets you punch above your weight.*
- *Hire for attitude, train for skill. Fire fast when needed; always be recruiting for the future.*
- *Great service is obsession-level work—always on, always solving.*
- *Cash flow is survival: deliver, invoice, collect, stretch payments, and then raise more.*
- *Dilution hurts but running out of money hurts more—optimize for increasing long-term enterprise value.*

4 Scaling to the Next Level

How to not just become bigger, but better.

4.1 The Next Phase

Building a business is a long and continuous process, and one thing is for sure: It is never finished.

But there are distinct phases in the journey. After the initial start-up phase of figuring out the basics, fighting for survival, and grinding away, the "scaling" phase begins.

For Blue Wireless, this was around 2020, five years into our adventure, when we took the first steps to expand outside of the Asia Pacific region. Our minds had to stretch beyond the daily operational challenges into questions like strategy, processes, organization, and how we could grow without going crazy or burning out (or broke).

Scaling is not just about becoming bigger; it is about becoming better so you can manage the business more efficiently and effectively. You need to grow revenue and margin faster than cost and head count, so you can generate profit and make the business sustainable in the long term. Scaling is also about making the business gradually independent from the founders, because you cannot keep "grinding away" indefinitely. Joop and I certainly did not want to work for eternity. We wanted to build a business to a level where it was future-proof, so it would offer real value for future buyers. And lastly, scaling is also about stopping certain things, making choices, and, in some cases, firing people.

Different types of businesses have different life cycles and scale differently. Technology businesses, for instance, require an enormous amount of time and investment up front to develop the unique software, hardware, or intellectual property (IP) needed. But once established, these can be reproduced in large numbers. SAAS (software as a service) companies have demonstrated this clearly, where software subscriptions can scale almost unlimitedly.

In the service business where Blue Wireless operated, our initial investment was limited, and our "IP" was developed along the way as we figured out how to sell, deliver, and support our services around the world. Service businesses are notoriously hard to scale, but there were some key areas that really made the difference for us: business strategy, the customer journey, the business process, automation, and, of course, people.

4.2 THE BUSINESS STRATEGY

Our sales and product strategy evolved quite a bit over the first few years, from the early gimmick of "Internet Access via a 4G Router" to "Wireless Network Solutions for Corporates," which in our minds was a very professional and appealing position. Our coverage ambitions also grew, as we pitched "service across sixteen countries in Asia Pacific"—although the reality was that the majority of our services were deployed in Singapore and Australia.

Our competencies and capabilities were growing fast. Our solutions included 5G/LTE technology, but we also did cabling projects, sold equipment, sold SIM cards, and provided event Wi-Fi. We served a wide range of use cases, from temporary events to solar farms to student housing to remote locations. And we served a wide range of customers: from small businesses to service providers and from government to large corporates. We were shooting at everything that came at us and were keen to show how versatile our technology was, how flexible we were as a company, and how our services could benefit everyone. We could do it all.

Joop and I at a BT partner event, Kuala Lumpur, Malaysia, 2017

The problem was that while the top line was growing, the bottom line was not. Payroll, inventory, rent, and every other imaginable expense ballooned as our activities grew. We were on our way to becoming a victim of our own success. While we were very busy, the reality was that it was a patchwork of activities with limited synergies and no economies of scale.

As we did more and more things, it started dawning on me that we had to discipline ourselves to only focus on activities where we could create repeatable solutions and long-term value. This was clearly in 5G/LTE access for the international corporate segment—a segment Joop and I had served throughout our careers and felt the most affinity with. The segment offered long-term contracts (thirty-six months was no exception, compared to the local customers who wanted solutions for three to six months) and volume (the number of locations was usually dozens and sometimes hundreds, compared to a handful for local customers). The only issue was that decision-making and rollout times, both from end customers and the global service providers (GSPs) that served them, were excruciatingly slow. In addition, they demanded global coverage, strict service levels, and mountains of paperwork, which we could not yet meet.

We felt stuck between two worlds. We needed the short-term quick orders that would give us a paycheck next month, and at the same time, we had to build the long-term capability that would only generate new income quarters from now. So, we did what is metaphorically referred to as "changing engines on an airplane while flying."

We kept our patchwork of local customers and solutions in Singapore and Australia running while we expanded our global capabilities across the Asia Pacific, Europe, and the Americas to serve our future segment of global corporates.

Joop on the way to another installation to enable crew Wi-Fi for Carnival Cruises, Sydney 2019

The cash flow from these off-strategy activities helped us remain afloat. One such project was for a company called Scape Student Housing in Australia, where Joop acted as fractional chief information officer for almost two years. Through the personal connection Joop maintained with the founders, we were able to lead the internal IT infrastructure for several apartment buildings, incorporating structured cabling, switches, high-speed fiber Internet access, hundreds of Wi-Fi access points, and more. Because of the personal trust and the fact that property developers treat these elements as infrastructure investment, we were able to charge upfront, giving us much needed cash flow. This was a welcome relief compared to most of our other services, which were charged monthly and only after completion. Scape was one of our most profitable projects during the early years and gave us the financial runway to build the long-term business.

But not every strategic variation was successful. Optimism can lead you into projects that drain cash and distract from your main mission. One such example was equipment sales.

Looking for more ways to generate short-term income, we had the idea of not only renting wireless routers to customers as a service but also selling them to those who preferred to own them; it seemed like a simple expansion. We already used the routers ourselves, had technical experience, and carried a good reputation, and we believed there was a clear demand ahead of us. When our router provider Cradlepoint struggled to establish themselves in Asia, we offered to become their distributor, and they agreed.

We created a separate legal entity, called it "Go Wireless," and gave it a wider appeal to potentially sell anything wireless—targeting business customers who preferred a do-it-yourself approach. We designed a website and logo with a different color scheme (yellow, as it contrasted nicely with blue) and established a whole separate business process. The team and I spent hundreds of hours and tens of thousands of dollars building this separate business. My long-term thinking was that we would build up two separate companies and potentially sell each of them, thereby creating an even bigger exit opportunity.

Reality was less glamorous. While we did manage to sell a few hundred thousand dollars over time, having another business with a different process was distracting for our customers and for us internally. We spent too much time developing new things while we should have been focusing on what we already had and making that better. Rather than stopping the business segment once we realized this, I doubled down in a stubborn "never give up" fashion. More about this adventure and how it ended in the next chapter about decision-making.

So, in conclusion, what was the lesson from trying all those variations of the Blue Wireless strategy? Simple: you don't know until you have tried it. Strategic 'planning' is a contradiction, or as they say in the military "No plan survives first contact with the enemy". Some things work, some things don't, key is to build on opportunities and not to go down the wrong path for too long, as you'll run out of energy and money.

* * *

One element of the business strategy is the pricing strategy and this is where entrepreneurs often struggle. Unless you have something truly unique and you have complete pricing freedom, most likely there is something in the market where customers compare your product or service to. For Blue Wireless there were two comparison points: the price of fixed line broadband and those of mobile phone plans and that's where the struggle was. Allow me to explain.

Ultimately, what we delivered was an internet broadband service, only we didn't use ADSL or Fibre or other fixed line alternatives, but 4G/5G, and the latter was what most people recognized from their mobile phone plans.

As business broadband services were priced usually in the 100-200 Singapore Dollar month range, we tried to match our pricing to that level. However, mobile phone plans where much cheaper and most consumers paid around 30 to 50. The perception that our service should be priced at the 'mobile' level was a tough one to break.

But we persisted in our pricing strategy and tried to increase the value which we provided to customers at the higher price level through better equipment, on-site support and maximum flexibility. Our service was famously 'all inclusive' which meant customers were never hit with extra bills and not 'nickel and dimed' for every single variation or request.

And it worked well, both for customers, who received ultimate peace of mind, and for us, as it made our invoicing much simpler! We certainly didn't have the billing capabilities to keep track of small amounts, add-ons and monthly usage variations, so our fixed pricing model killed two birds with one stone: customers never received 'bill-shock' and we kept our invoicing (and thus collections) simple and consistent. And that is a very valuable element of the next concept: the customer journey.

4.3 THE CUSTOMER JOURNEY

The "customer journey" is something every business should fully understand and map out in detail, so customers have an outstanding experience from start to finish. From learning about the product or service through marketing to the sales process, ordering, receiving the goods or services, in-life support, billing, and payments—a smooth, "frictionless" experience is what one should aim to deliver as a business.

The reality is less smooth. For a new start-up company offering a new service like Blue Wireless, it took many, many customer journeys, loaded with friction, before we learned how to explain the service, what options to offer, what their preferred ordering methods were, how to communicate installations, and how to support and invoice them. And each customer seemed to tell us something different. Remember the paper invoices and checks? That was a customer requirement.

The customer journey starts with the sales process. Success in sales does not mean closing a large, single deal but continuously repeating a process to generate improved outcomes over time. It is a numbers game. Most people in corporate sales know the "factor ten," which means that for every one hundred leads, there are probably only ten real opportunities that eventually lead to one actual closed deal. To be successful in sales, the trick is to perfect your process and reduce those ten real opportunities to five, or even two, because you simply do not have the money, time, and energy to live with a one-in-one hundred close rate.

This is where a "sales formula" helps to map out the critical success factors or "levers" in the sales process. This varies depending on your type of market, customers, and product, but in our process of selling business services to multinationals via sales channels, our formula looked roughly like this:

$$Productization \times Contacts\ Known \times Attention$$
$$= Opportunities \times \frac{Value}{Price} = Orders$$

Allow me to explain:

- **Productization.** We sold most of our services not directly to multinationals but via GSPs who functioned as our sales channels. The first step was for those channels to adopt our service. It's like a retailer deciding to carry your brand and "make it their own" or "productize" it. For a start-up, getting your product adopted is a major task with a long sales cycle. There are many people to convince and endless objections to overcome on why they should not use your service. For some, it took us six months to get adopted; for others, six years. If you follow a channel sales model, this is crucial to your success—but it is only the first step.
- **Contacts Known.** Even if you are adopted and "in the catalogue," then what? If the sales staff within the channel do not know you, you still will not sell any services. For consumer products or e-commerce, this might be different, but for enterprise sales, the sales teams are a crucial factor. Navigating these companies and getting to the right teams is hard. GSPs are complex organizations and many actively try to discourage you or stonewall you when you try to contact or build relations with their sales teams. And there is constant churn, with people changing positions or leaving. Getting to those folks is

essential—that is step two after getting accepted by the product and procurement teams.
- **Attention.** Once you know the people you need to work with, how do you get and keep their attention? They are busy and have tons of vendors clamoring for their time and a wide range of products and services to sell. Staying "top of mind" is your next challenge—that is what will generate opportunities when they decide to put your product or service in front of their customers.
- **Opportunities.** Once there is an opportunity with a customer, the actual sale starts. Within a channel sales opportunity, the levers you have are limited. You are not communicating with the customer directly and often do not fully understand their organization, timeline, buying criteria, politics, etc. So you must work through your sales channel and create maximum value to increase your chances of success, fully aware that the influence you have on the outcome is limited.
- **Value and Price.** The main lever you have is offering maximum value at an optimal price. Offering value requires you to understand what they value, so you can increase those elements. Often, however, price is the only thing that sales channels are interested in, and you get endless requests for reductions, discounts, and waivers.

Putting pen to paper and mapping out the various elements in the sales process was the first step in improving the customer journey. Many more parts followed: from how to quote, how to support, how to invoice, and so forth.

4.4 THE GLOBAL EXPANSION

By 2019 we were operating from three countries: Singapore, Australia, and Malaysia. We registered entities in Hong Kong, Thailand, and New Zealand to enable more local coverage across the region, and our team and operations grew steadily.

New office opening in Singapore in September 2018

We felt really comfortable with the region, which was all in one time zone, and Joop and I had a good understanding of how each country operated. Singapore and Sydney were the main centers, and local business grew steadily.

We always felt strongly about creating a good office environment and we probably spend above average compared to other (bootstrapped) start-ups. Lots of branding throughout the office, good materials, ample kitchen- and food options, really something where we and everyone else would feel comfortable spending time.

We also had tons of social activities, starting with team lunches, 'pot-luck' gatherings and after work beer sessions to elaborate team building activities. We tried to find something which brought people not only together, but also out of their comfort zone and ideally something competitive. The list was long: from VR laser games, beach sailing and dragon boating to creative painting sessions, indoor skydiving and of course several MasterChef cooking sessions.

We always resisted the demand for 'home-working' and pushed people to work in the office as we felt it lacked the opportunity for learning, quick decision making and camaraderie which is so essential during a start-up phase. This was well accepted in the early years, but the Covid-19 period changed people's perspective and post pandemic we allowed for up two days of home working for staff once they spend 6 moths with the company and proved they could handle the responsibility. To this day I firmly believe that home working - despite the travel time benefits - is not as productive as office working and that people are missing out of the social interaction – spending even more time at home isolated. But that's my old age speaking.

Our start in Malaysia was quite good from an office perspective, but less successful business-wise as we struggled to convince customers to adopt our type of "managed services," but customers generally opted to source just equipment and local data plans and put things together themselves. One of the reasons for this was the low cost of labor and relative high level of education, which meant most customers had their own network engineers to manage IT activities, and they could often do it faster and cheaper than us. After a good year of trying win local business, we changed tactics and started the transformation of our Kuala Lumpur office towards a technical support hub for the region. The availability of well skilled and affordable network engineers made this an ideal back office.

Our Global Support Centre, Kuala Lumpur, Malaysia, 2020

At that moment, we still had a gap between the service levels we promised our customers (including 24/7 support) and what we actually delivered (mostly Joop and Syam being on standby during nights and weekends). The "Global Support Centre" or GSC was born and during the following years this proved to be a very important capability to help support our global expansion.

As we gained more traction with our GSP customers, the questions about services outside of the Asia Pacific region became ever more prevalent. While we were concentrating on delivering our services in remote places like Myanmar and Mongolia, customers were enquiring about Belgium and Germany.

The discussions Joop and I had about expanding outside of the Asia Pacific region became more frequent and intense in early 2019 as we realized this was a potential game changer for the business. Could we truly become a 'global' business?

However, we were already stretched across multiple countries and our services were far from perfect. Expanding outside of our region would spread ourselves even thinner, create time-zone challenges and cost more money which we didn't have.

We had had longer deliberation with our board members to prepare them for more fundraising in the future and by that summer, we felt confident we were ready for the step. As Joop and I are both from the Netherlands, it was a natural step to start there, and we had our network of friends and family and basics like bank accounts to get started.

But despite our personal connections, operating in the Netherlands felt initially like a "far away" region for us, and so it was good to have someone truly local to manage the daily activities. In late 2019 one of my old university friends Pieter joined the team and lead the development of Blue Wireless in the Netherlands.

After a short period of working from the kitchen table and borrowing someone else's workspace, our first office was established in the Stoflab on the Figeeterrein in Haarlem. The setup was basic and the second floor accessible only by stairs, which the DHL courier didn't really appreciate as the number of packages increased, but we were in business!

Our first office in the Netherlands, Stoflab, Haarlem, August 2020

The first few hires in the Netherlands were a little hit-and-miss as we faced the same challenges initially in Singapore—we had little to offer staff and show for. But after twelve months, we gradually got into a rhythm of sales and delivery, and slowly we started to look like a functioning company.

As customers continued to push us "westwards," we made the step to establish in the USA in early 2021. Again, we relied on our network of contacts to find someone to take ownership of establishing operations in a new location.

Opening of our US office, Richmond, Virginia, June 2021

Michael and I used to work together in Expereo Singapore years before and was brave enough to take up the challenge.

Similar to our setup in the Netherlands where our first office was biking distance from Pieter's home, here we started in Richmond, Virginia, where Michael resided. Also similar to the Netherlands, we chose to get started in a start-up community building, which gave us all the basics. Finding locations with expansion options proved to be a good strategy, because, since 2021, we moved two more times within the same building. Every one to two years we needed an office a bit bigger to accommodate the growing team and need for storage.

Opening of our UK office, Chester, England, 2023

The last of the international expansions was into the UK in 2022. While relatively close to the Netherlands when looking at it from a global perspective, the UK proved to be quite different—it very much functioned as gateway to the

EU. As the volume in the UK continued to grow, so did the cost of shipping, travel, and taxes, and thus it was time to go local. Here we followed the same playbook of finding a good, local leader who would build local operations and a team. Through our network we found Andrew. Testing his wife's patience with initially starting our local shipping operations in their spare bedroom, we soon took the step to establish a small office in Chester, England. And as volume grew, he built a team, moved to bigger offices, and put our UK operations on the map.

By 2023, we had built a truly global network of offices and people and we were able to service customers in each of the main regions: AsiaPac, Europe and the Americas. Revenues were still largely generated in AsiaPac region, but Europe was rapidly catching up and the Americas was starting its own acceleration and by end of 2025, half of our business was generated from Europe, while AsiaPac and Americas did a quarter each. But the global expansion not only allowed us to significantly grow revenue, it fundamentally changed our service offering and business process.

4.5 THE BUSINESS PROCESS

As we were scaling our physical presence around the world, the complexity of our operations dramatically increased, and the initial way of working in our small teams didn't work anymore. The advantage of being small is great—everyone, from sales to delivery to invoicing to support, knew every customer, everyone pretty much knew what was going on, and being in the same office, we could easily check in.

As we grew to more locations, this level of familiarity was no longer a given, and we needed to seriously think about designing a business process.

A business process is the internal machinery that allows you to repeatedly deliver what the customer needs at each stage of the journey. Like an iceberg, the customer only sees the small tip above water (someone shows up to install a router at their location), but not the massive amount of work underwater (the router had to be quoted, sold, bought, shipped, configured, tested, sent to an engineer, scheduled for delivery, invoiced, collected, and so on).

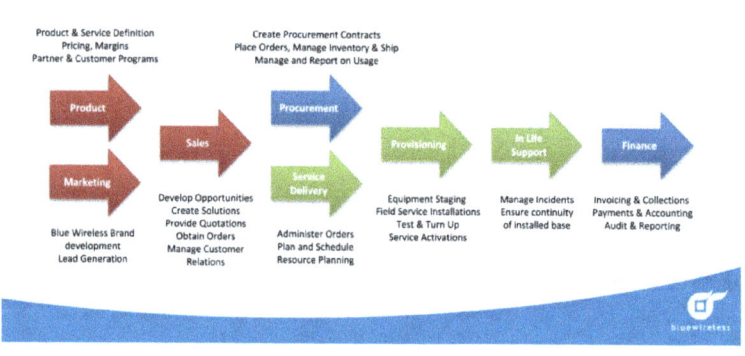

Our first written-down business process in 2020.

The business process gradually grew into different disciplines and departments, each with its own specialty that needed to be deepened and developed. A good business process is one of the pillars of long-term business success, and at Blue Wireless, we spent an enormous amount of time and effort improving ours.

We did not fully understand the importance of this at the start. Initially, we focused heavily on technology. Our technical team spent endless hours trying to find the right options and ways to get services working. Of course, this was essential to keep customers happy. Even in our marketing communications, we profiled ourselves as offering technical breakthroughs and new technologies until we realized that most customers cared less about the bits and bytes and more about how we got things done.

Customers wanted to know how we managed to deliver on our bold claim that we could install a service anywhere in the Asia Pacific region in three working days. What method or "magic" were we using, while others needed weeks? Gradually, we became aware that we were, at heart, a service company, offering a consistent experience we could deliver repeatedly. That became one of our unique selling points.

As we started to focus on repeatable service instead of doing individual projects, the order volume continued to increase. Dozens became hundreds, and in December 2019, we reached one of our first magic milestones of completing one thousand installations. We were extremely proud.

Even in our fundraising efforts we stressed this to prospective investors as one of the key values and differentiators. As they probed for our "secret," we increasingly started talking about our "service delivery model," similar to McDonald's, which can churn out a consistent experience around the world for anyone with a fast-food craving. And like McDonald's, we started with our first process documents and training manuals.

Celebrating our one thousandth installation in December 2019.

We created manuals for everything under the sun: pricing, quoting, ordering, configuring, shipping, instructing engineers, site surveys, testing, handover documents, support manuals—everything from how to pick up the phone to which naming convention to use for stickers on routers. We moved from creating "'The Bible," "Operations Manuals," and "Knowledge Bases" to implementing "Zoho Learn" to using online courses.

But the moment we wrote something down it was outdated because someone had come up with something better. That's when we learned that it was impossible for people to keep up with all the instructions and details that make up a business process. Ideally, systems should be smart enough to guide people to do the work correctly.

4.6 THE AUTOMATION

Automation is a no-brainer if you want to grow and scale. But you cannot automate if you do not have a business process, and you cannot have a business process if you do not understand the customer journey. That is the challenge: You cannot automate what you do not know, and the only way to learn is to live through it.

So here is some controversial advice: Do not go out on day one and subscribe to a professional business process package like Salesforce. We did this in our first year at Blue Wireless and never used it. We were keen to become professional quickly and subscribing to an expensive and complex tool gave us a false sense of competence. We wasted around 3,000 Singapore dollars on an early subscription, never used it properly, and canceled after a year. (Subsequently, Salesforce sent us a letter of demand from their lawyer for the mandatory second-year subscription, which we never paid despite numerous calls and threats.)

There is a difference between software for specific tasks and software for the wider business process. Software for specific tasks automates a particular function—accounting, email marketing, etc. We used those successfully, from Mailchimp to Xero to NetCloud.

The difficulty usually comes with the larger packages you use to automate a broad business process, which can impact the whole organization for years to come. The challenge is that your business process is still fluid at the early stages, and you need maximum flexibility to adjust your offers to customers and your way of doing things internally.

My recommendation for early startups: Use standard Excel sheets for as long as you can manage. Not only do you save the headache of implementation, but you also save time and gain flexibility. You can add, delete, or start all over in a minute.

At Blue Wireless, we ran our entire internal operations in Excel for a good four years until the scale and volume became a real challenge, and we decided that it was finally time to automate properly. The Excel method was tedious, but it allowed us to learn what information was important in the process and what was not. We called the method "True North," referring to how navigators like pilots or sailors try to work out the true course, although few people in the company actually understood the meaning. As volume grew, the method became unworkable as we constantly had to rekey information and had too many people working in the same sheets.

After the Salesforce mistake, we made another similar mistake by buying into a package that promised to do it all: Microsoft Dynamics. This time we thought we were smarter by engaging a software integrator to do the development and implementation. After several frustrating months, we pulled the plug. Total cost: roughly 12,000 Singapore dollars down the drain.

By that time, our business process was functioning reasonably well, but trying to replicate that process inside such software turned out to be like fitting a square peg into a round hole. Because we had a consultant as an in-between, explaining the business process to a third party and then having that party make the changes was an enormous challenge. Discouraged, we went back to our Excel sheets, which by then were literally unmanageable—full of errors, duplicates, and multiple versions created by different staff.

Third time lucky? Yes. By 2020, our third attempt was finally successful when we selected Zoho as a package that allowed us to customize it to our needs and evolve over time.

Here is what we learned:

- **Flexibility is key.** As with many things in a growing business, you need to balance scale with flexibility. When selecting packages, choose those with maximum flexibility to configure, adjust, and program. If it requires a permanent consultant to operate, stay away; you need to master it yourself.

- **Master your software.** Just as with hiring people and winning customers, you need to master your software and get your hands dirty. That means hours of study, tinkering, and trial and error to know the package inside out. Besides yourself, you will probably need someone with software development skills in your organization to support this.

- **Your business process leads.** Most software has built-in functions and templates based on "best practices" and tries to pull you into its way of doing things. Be stubborn. Develop the process you need, then configure the software around it.

- **Gradual improvement.** As with every other part of the business, software development is about gradual improvement. From the minimum viable product to sprints to releases, you make it better step by step—and accept that it will never be perfect.
- **Integration.** Choose software that plays well with other packages. This is now standard in the software world, but check which integrations exist and which are planned.

Zoho became the foundation for our internal business process, but it really became effective once we started integrating it with other systems, notably Xero for invoicing and NetCloud for technical operations.

Xero had been our accounting package from the early days and worked well for a small business, with maximum flexibility for invoices, bills, payroll, and accounting—pretty much all we needed at the start. But as our volume of customers and services grew, with ever more variables like different plans and usage, the time it took to get invoices out went from hours to days each month.

As Zoho became more functional, we worked on establishing a link between the Zoho service module and the Xero invoice module. "DeskUtility" was created by our only application developer: a simple batch program that ran on your desktop and exported service lines from Zoho into the invoice lines in Xero. We were elated—it saved us dozens of hours of rekeying every month—until, once again, the sheer volume and billing variations made it unworkable. We had to develop a better, more intelligent, more connected method. "BillTown" was born.

By that time, we had two developers. The first proper cloud-based application they built was "SIM City" (for SIM card management), and BillTown became the second. Many more developments and integrations followed.

By 2023, we had automated the full internal business process from order intake to delivery to support to invoicing. We had a stable platform capable of handling hundreds of orders per month and managing thousands of services. On the external customer journey, we still lagged expectations, but we could get by with some manual work (for example, sending manual quotations by email). By 2025, our IT applications team had grown to three staff and started working on a true middleware layer: enabling APIs between systems, ensuring access control, managing data storage, and overseeing security across the wider IT environment.

All of this—strategy, processes, and automation—created the infrastructure for scale. But in the end, it was the people and culture that turned that infrastructure into a living, breathing business.

4.7 People Make the Difference

While our business process and its automation were huge contributors to our success, the much bigger element was the organization and culture that started to emerge, almost without us realizing it.

In our daily work, Joop and I always led from the front, working hard, giving the right example. In the early years, literally every single task in the business could be done by either of us—and often by both. We faced issues head-on, were brutally honest about options, and solved problems where we could, even if it took extra hours, unconventional methods, or calling in favors from our network. We just got shit done.

As we hired more people, this became an example that resonated. The Dutch "directness," combined with the Singaporean "sense of urgency" and Australian "unfazedness," formed the foundation of a unique Blue Wireless culture that started to take shape.

Culture

After I hired a new marketing manager in the Netherlands in late 2021, we started brainstorming on a much-needed brand refresh. We concluded that people should be the main brand element of Blue Wireless. Not routers, not technology, not even our global coverage or service model—our people truly made the difference.

The rebrand that followed, and which is still active today, prominently features our own staff in all materials. From LinkedIn posts to websites and brochures, we have never used models or stock photography—only our own people telling the world what makes us unique. With that realization came the need to finally write down the specific values of Blue Wireless. Here they are:

- **We tell it like it is.** We know a thing or two about wireless solutions, but we'll always be straight with our customers and with each other. We communicate openly and directly and, as we value honesty, we welcome timely feedback to help us improve every day.

- **We evolve together.** We're in a dynamic field where technology evolves constantly, and we continuously improve our services and processes. We grow as a company and as a team, and we help our customers with their own wireless journeys.

- **We reach for the smiles.** Our customers' happiness is serious business for us, as is helping them succeed in this wireless world. But also, it's important for *us*: Enjoy the work and get a smile on your colleague's face. Our people make the difference, and we go the extra mile to get things done.

- **We think global.** Our customers are global and so is our team—a melting pot of cultures, ideas, and skills from around the world. This allows and inspires us to always think and act globally in our processes, solutions, and ways of working.

Directness is clearly captured in the first value. Continuous improvement is built into the second and prepares staff for the fact that things are constantly changing at Blue Wireless. The third is a cheeky combination of having fun together but not at the expense of our customers, who are the primary ones we serve.

Team building at iFly, Singapore, 2019

The last one confirms both our business strategy—serving global customers—and the need for globally minded team members.

But besides the formal definition of our values and culture, we just wanted people to have a good time together: making sure they felt good about their work and having fun during office hours, but also afterwards. Many friendships started at work, and people went out for drinks, dinner, and sports. Our team building activities covered anything from painting to climbing to beach sailing to *MasterChef* competitions. And they were absolutely amazing.

Team building at iFly, Netherlands, 2021

While "diversity" has become a politically loaded word over the last years, Blue Wireless was enormously diverse right from the start, and the mix of backgrounds, languages, skills, and perspectives has truly made us stronger, better, and "funner" as a business.

Organization

To maintain great people and a strong culture, the organization itself needs to be managed and evolve constantly. Until the seventh year of the business, we did not have any HR manager or much of a formal organization structure. Joop and I recruited, hired, fired, and managed staff directly ourselves. I believe this was a key ingredient for our later success.

Roughly half the staff reported to Joop and the other half to me, as we split the company by discipline. Joop's half was mostly operations, technology, and support, while I focused on sales, finance, marketing, product, and procurement. There was still a lot of overlap, as we were both involved in many aspects of the business.

As we approached fifty staff, the "span of control" for both of us became far too large to manage people effectively. We needed a first management layer. Building that first layer was not easy. We tried to promote people from within and see if they could rise to the challenge. Being a manager for the first time is hard: You suddenly manage people and carry more responsibility. But if you step up to this challenge and nurture, reward, and motivate them—they will be the engine room for your next level of growth.

As we started to formalize the management layer, we also began assigning stock appreciation rights (SARs), also known as stock options, allowing early staff to benefit from an exit based on how much the share price appreciated during their tenure. It is a simple and straightforward method without the complications of actual share ownership, taxes, etc. Once we exited in 2023, it paid handsomely to those early managers. Issuing SARs does not dilute actual share ownership, but it does create a liability for the company to pay bonuses later once there is an exit, lowering the potential payout to founders and shareholders. We reserved a maximum of 10 percent of the total exit payout for SARs payments, which is a common percentage for venture start-ups.

In hindsight, we had many good hires, and many staff had fulfilling and rewarding careers over the years. But we certainly made mistakes too. Like many other things that go wrong in the business, the key learning is to correct mistakes as swiftly as you can. For people matters this is doubly important: People who are not performing, are toxic, or not aligned with the business are not just dead weight and costly—they can negatively influence others, customers, and the business overall. Firing people is hard, as the following examples show.

The second salesperson I hired (and fired) in Singapore was a good learning moment. Keen to hire a woman alongside our first male account manager, I hired someone who had some sales experience but turned out not to be as sophisticated in her manners as she came across during the interview. Without an HR manager or sophisticated process, I made an offer after the first interview. But three days into the job, the late arrivals, frequent smoke breaks, and unprofessional behavior started to get on my nerves. As quickly as I had hired her, I decided to let her go.

The next evening, I called her, explained the situation, and told her she did not need to come back to work. As the process was quite fast and abrupt, I made a generous offer to pay her salary for the remainder of the month, hoping this would settle things. It did not. The following days were full of late-night calls from her—crying, pleading for her job, emotionally blackmailing me like a disgruntled ex-girlfriend. Eventually she relented and picked up her personal items after hours, but it was a stressful few days and my first wake-up call on how difficult firing can be.

That was actually one of the easier staff decisions. A much more difficult decision came three years later, when I had to let go my long-term friend Pieter who had managed our business in the Netherlands since its inception in late 2019. That was hard.

Poor performance or bad behavior is easy to recognize and can be a clear reason for dismissal. With more senior managers like Pieter, it is often about alignment with the vision and the business—much harder to quantify and decide on.

In our case, we tried to evolve the organization into a global team all working via the same processes and systems, which was different from how we grew the company up to that point. Our initial growth in Singapore, Australia, and the Netherlands had been largely independent. We shared the vision, brand, and product offering, but the execution was left to the local teams. This allowed us to start quickly in each new country and use whatever worked best locally. Pieter had done a stellar job in the Netherlands: scaling from a one-man setup working from home to finding customers, suppliers, and staff, and turning it into a fully functioning operation.

But as the business grew, I realized it would be difficult to scale Blue Wireless if each local team did things differently, especially as customers expected a consistent global experience. We started to evolve our systems and processes towards a more centralized approach. Our vision was long-term scale and global consistency; the local focus was short-term profit optimization.

The change was not received and the classic "HQ versus branch office" tension surfaced. Directions were ignored, focus was not the same as before, and our weekly catch-up calls became tense and full of conflict. Sitting in Singapore with only occasional visits to the Netherlands, I could only do so much. It felt like two captains were steering the same ship.

The decision to not continue his contract was difficult and did not happen overnight, causing me several sleepless nights. Often, in difficult situations, there are two parts: the mental decision and the execution. The mental part is often the hardest, as you weigh all the options and pros and cons. It is essential to have the decision fully formed before you move to the execution, which followed a few weeks later when I visited in person in Amsterdam.

In hindsight, parting ways was the right decision. We needed to evolve the organization and have everyone rowing in the same direction. The months after his departure were tough, as we tried to implement new global processes while effectively running without local management. It cost me a friendship, but it was a crucial decision—without it, we would not have been able to progress as a company.

Getting Out of the Way

As the organization evolves, so does the role of the founders. In the beginning, all decisions and much of the execution are done by you. Once the organization and processes are better established, you work more on an "exception basis"—things come to you only when something is unclear, broken, missing, or needs improvement. That still adds up to hundreds of things per week.

The reality is that while organization and automation allow you to handle more volume and scale, as a founder you are still deeply involved operationally. Getting to the next level—letting go of operations and working on truly strategic matters—requires mental discipline, which even today, as I write this book, I have not fully mastered.

Mark Zuckerberg once said in an interview, "The hardest thing about running a company is that you don't get to do most of the things yourself anymore." We love to do things ourselves so they are done the right way. But organizational growth requires more than delegation and structure; it also requires preparing the next level of leaders to "carry the flame" and act as "protectors of the culture." I did not invent that last term—one of the senior managers told me that's how he saw his role, and it vividly illustrates how important culture is in any business.

Every year we celebrated Blue Wireless's birthday, August 2022

Being involved in daily operations creates bottlenecks. It shapes the need and desire of people to make decisions for themselves or within their team. With the boss cc'd in emails or present in meetings, staff often adopt a "wait and see" attitude, waiting for you to decide. For those who want to move fast, your presence becomes frustrating.

The best practice is to set clear objectives for individuals or teams, define the high-level process to follow, and let people do their jobs. The challenge is to define these objectives, track them, and refine them. Often this is a discovery process for founders: You need to write down what people specifically need to achieve, trying to make it specific, measurable, achievable, realistic, and time-bound (the famous SMART method). You want people to be busy—but busy with the right things, where they have the most impact.

This takes practice. You will probably switch between different intervals (monthly, quarterly) and approaches (informal chats, written emails, dedicated systems) over time. Whatever method you choose, keep communicating what you expect from your team, both at the company level and at the individual manager level.

Getting out of the way is the first step towards succession planning—preparing the next generation of leaders to take over the management of the business. That is something you need to start planning for early: Identify staff who are up for the challenge and nurture them for the next step. Your task now is to work yourself out of a job.

Key Learnings

- *Scaling means becoming better, not just bigger—while reducing dependency on the founders.*
- *Strategic focus is essential—doing everything creates noise and is not sustainable.*
- *Customer journeys are learned through friction—real-world feedback refines your sales, delivery, and support approach.*
- *Automate only after you understand the process—flexible tools and hands-on mastery beat early big-software purchases.*
- *Culture and people outperform everything else—how you behave as founders becomes how the company behaves.*
- *Founders must eventually get out of the way; building leaders who can steer the business is the ultimate scaling milestone.*

5 ESSENTIAL SKILLS

Skills and mindsets for the entrepreneur

5.1 Tools of the Trade

Are entrepreneurs born or made? Can it be taught? Do you need to go to business school? What are the skills you really need as an entrepreneur?

Entrepreneurship is generally a mix of certain character traits and a set of skills you can learn over time. As explained in one of the earlier chapters, since I was young, I was always active, curious, and loved to create things, but as a young adult, I never thought of myself as a businessman or entrepreneur. I probably didn't even know what the word really meant until well into college.

What I did have were some useful traits: strong self-motivation, resilience, and a love of taking risks. That turned out to be a good foundation for dealing with the challenges of building a business.

My years in corporate life taught me most of my business and financial skills: strategic planning, how to manage customers and suppliers, and above all, how to manage people. I was lucky to get that solid foundation before jumping into my own venture.

Starting with Joop as cofounder, we effectively had double the skills. Where I lacked operational experience, he filled in. When it came to financial planning and marketing, I took the lead. That balance helped us move much faster than either of us could have alone.

So, there isn't a single formula for what you need to be successful as an entrepreneur. But after ten years on the job, some skills clearly stood out as essential to surviving the journey:

- Become Resilient
- Good decision-making
- Continuous improvement
- Time management
- Endless Creativity

These five skills became the core of my own "entrepreneur's toolkit," and the rest of this chapter walks through each of them.

5.2 Skill 1: Become Resilient

Eric Idles sings the song "Always look on the bright side of life" in *Monty Python's Life of Brian* as he is nailed to the cross. If you've never seen it, watch that scene on YouTube: It's funny, absurd, and greatly uplifting.

It captures a kind of stoic, stiff-upper-lip spirit often associated with the British. It also applies nicely to entrepreneurs: No matter what happens, don't let things keep you down for long.

Keeping your spirits up is a key trait for any entrepreneur, and both Joop and I had plenty of it. Whether we were born that way or learned it over the years, we very rarely stayed miserable, no matter what struggles we faced. We shared a similar sense of humor—happy to ridicule ourselves and see the funny side of almost any situation.

And as mentioned before, we also loved our gin and tonics, which helped us relax after a long day, and more than once they led to spirited debates at home or in a bar—and the conversation always circled back to Blue Wireless.

As we hired more people, we never explicitly selected on humor (or drinking habits), but we did select people we could connect and laugh with. Even across different nationalities, ages, and backgrounds—from young guys to older mothers—we found that we could have fun with almost everyone in the company, and people could laugh with each other. I think it was part of our culture: We let people be themselves, be a bit silly, and not feel like they had to behave in a stiff "corporate" way.

But even on my own, whenever I had a setback or felt down or didn't want to get out of bed, I often used humor to pick myself up. Being a movie buff, I used scenes and quotes as my personal pep-talk toolkit.

Some of my favorites (showing my age here):

- "You're gonna need a bigger boat"—*Jaws*
- "Just keep swimming,"—*Finding Nemo*
- "Show me the money!"—*Jerry Maguire*
- "Failure is not an option!"—*Apollo 13* (which I later flipped around at work to "Failure is an option" to stop people fussing over small mistakes and just move on)

These little quotes are silly on the surface, but they gave me the quick mental pickup to keep moving and overcome the daily obstacles that never seem to relent: chasing customers, chasing payments, someone didn't show, something didn't work, someone quit, systems failed—you named it, it happened daily. And you get trained to deal with them like playing Tetris, squaring problems away one at a time.

But some problems were externally imposed on us like Covid-19. I was mostly annoyed rather than scared as I thought, "I don't have time for this crap, I got a business to build!" and so I carried on as per normal, and we doubled down, despite all the restrictions imposed on us. Joop and I spent many days in quarantine isolation hotels following overseas trips to be able to continue our expansion plans.

It wasn't just humor, gin, or the "stiff upper lip" that helped us though. We genuinely embraced the challenges and were probably a little hooked on solving problems. Similar to a student who gets into the flow of solving endless mathematics equations, solving problems in a business can become addictive. Tackling a series of issues each day gives you a small dopamine hit every time you close one out.

And that's where the phrase 'onwards and upwards' started to come in. I'm not sure who first used it, but amongst Joop, myself, many of the early joiners and later managers, we used onwards and upwards as a battle cry to capture the spirit of always keep going, no matter what happens.

Resilience, for me, is that combination: being able to laugh, put things in perspective, take the hits, and come back the next day ready to solve the next round of problems. Once you learn to see problems as a series of puzzles rather than personal attacks or failures, you're already halfway there.

And that brings me to the second skill you need to master: good decision-making.

5.3 Skill 2: Make Better Decisions

As a leader, your most important job, day in and day out, is to make decisions. Some big, some small, but being decisive is essential to keep the business moving. The buck really does stop with you.

You're not only deciding on what you spend your own time and energy on. As the organization grows, your decisions are amplified: What you decide will direct dozens of people to work on things that can either advance or hold back the company. An entrepreneur who is afraid to decide is useless, and one who makes reckless decisions will drive the company into the ground.

Unlike larger companies where Joop and I used to work, we didn't have to worry much about politics. There was no need to get "buy-in" from committees, no endless meetings, no higher boss protecting or scolding us. That's both freeing and scary. It means you can move fast, but you also own the consequences.

Making decisions swiftly and rationally and communicating them clearly is key. Over the years, a few simple tools helped me in my daily decision-making:

Eisenhower Matrix

I practiced this for years before I learned it had a name: the Eisenhower Matrix. If you Google it, you'll find plenty of diagrams, but it boils down to sorting decisions and actions along two axes:

- Urgent / Not Urgent
- Important / Not Important

It's an incredibly simple but powerful way to prioritize your tasks, problems, and decisions.

Once things start scaling, your email inbox usually drives your daily work, and you can easily have hundreds of emails and dozens of topics demanding attention. So how do you decide what to do first?

- **Urgent and important.** These jump at you: customers not paying bills, staff about to quit, suppliers not delivering. These are fires to put out. Try not to have more than five to ten of these at any time.
- **Urgent and not important.** Noise that still needs to be handled: a customer asking about a small issue that could become a bigger problem later, for example. Clear these quickly using the "Four *D*" method I'll describe later in this chapter.
- **Not urgent but important.** This is the tricky quadrant. These are things like redesigning a process, choosing a new system, or planning the next big move. They are easy to postpone because solving small problems gives a nice dopamine rush. But if you delay these too long, you will not progress in your scaling. These need to be scheduled into weekly or quarterly planning.
- **Not urgent and not important.** Ignore or defer. It's perfectly fine not to solve every problem. "New expense claim system? Let's look at it next year." That goes here.

Another concept I like is the "lifespan of a decision": How long do you have to live with the consequences, especially if you get it wrong?

A social media post has a lifespan of hours or days. Do your best but don't overthink it.

Hiring someone or signing off on a big event or marketing campaign affects you for months or longer. Think more carefully.

Choosing a core technology or business system may stay with you for years. These decisions deserve a lot of time, debate, and data.

Adding Starlink to our portfolio was one of those long-lifespan decisions. Joop and I debated it for months. In hindsight, it was absolutely the right call and changed the course of the company for years, but it was not a decision to make lightly.

So how do you think through the harder decisions?

Six Thinking Hats

Most people in business have heard someone say, "Let's put our thinking caps on" or "You're wearing your black hat now." This comes from a book called *Six Thinking Hats* by Edward de Bono.

It's a framework for looking at a problem from different angles. These are the six "hats":

- **Green Hat**—Ideas, possibilities, creativity, out-of-the-box thinking

- **White Hat**—Facts, data, information, being as neutral as possible
- **Red Hat**—Intuition, gut feeling, emotions
- **Yellow Hat**—Optimism, benefits, and advantages
- **Black Hat**—Risks, weaknesses, what can go wrong
- **Blue Hat**—Process, structure, how to manage and control things

Most entrepreneurs, including me, tend to wear the green, red, and yellow hats by default: lots of ideas, gut feeling, and optimism. That energy is important—without it, you probably wouldn't have started a business in the first place.

But you need counterweight from the white, black, and blue hats: data, risk awareness, and process. For many founders, those ways of thinking don't come naturally, so you need people around you who bring those angles.

A good example was the product management at Blue Wireless. In the early days, we had a simple method: I "would sell it" and Joop "would make sure it worked." We even joked about this with customers, and they accepted it because we both took responsibility for the result.

As I got more salespeople under my wing and more engineers under Joop's, this model didn't work anymore. We needed to define upfront what exactly we could sell and under what conditions, so it could be delivered reliably. We needed real product management.

Product management is a curious discipline: A product manager is responsible for the whole customer journey and process but doesn't directly control all the teams involved. When you work in services, the list of things to define and scenarios to think through is long.

At first, I did the product management myself. I had tons of input and high-level ideas, but I forgot to define half of what happened during the service process. Luckily, our staff were flexible and empowered enough to fill in the gaps in real life, and we got by for a while. But as the team and footprint grew, "winging it" was no longer enough.

Then we hired Elvin Lim as product manager in late 2019. His character was very different from mine. Even though I thought he was making things too complicated and looking at too many negative scenarios, he was exactly what we needed. I brought the green and red hats; Elvin brought a lot of black and blue. Together, product development became balanced and well-managed.

The key lesson: Not every hat has equal weight in every decision, but you need all of them represented over time. In the end, the positive hats must win often enough—you still need to move forward and take risks—but the cautionary hats stop you from driving off a cliff.

We applied the same idea more broadly: tension between sales (positive, closing deals) and engineering (cautious, can it actually work?) is healthy, as long as it's managed. Over time, I became less involved in individual decisions as managers developed their own judgement and their own mix of hats.

We did give some guiding principles such as "Don't ask for permission, ask for forgiveness", which worked in many cases when you're unsure whether to move forward. Or another one when people came to ask for permission was "If the answer is yes, you don't ask", meaning, if you're doing the right thing for the company or the customer, there is no need to ask, just do it.

Joop and I said "yes" a lot and therefore we needed to learn the opposite.

Learning How to Say No

There are many more sophisticated tools for weighing decisions—decision matrices, cost-benefit analyses, and so on—but in a start-up, where you are constrained by everything, the 80/20 rule (the idea that 20 percent of things drive 80 percent of the results) is often the most practical tool.

For entrepreneurs with a positive outlook, it's hard to say no to new opportunities and even harder to stop things you've already started. Economists call this the "sunk cost fallacy": continuing to invest in something just because you've already put time or money into it, even when you should walk away.

We had several cases like this at Blue Wireless. A clear one was our e-commerce project.

Around year five, our customer base was changing. We were moving from small businesses towards larger enterprises and then to global service providers serving multinationals. Strategically, that shift was very successful: It drove our global expansion, profitability, and eventually our exit.

The global service provider / multinational segment represented more than 80 percent of our business and was growing. At the same time, we had a long tail of small customers that was shrinking. Serving small business is usually more expensive per dollar of revenue: They need more support, spend less, and are less structured.

The rational choice would have been to let that small-business segment slowly fade and focus on the 80 percent. Instead, green hat firmly on, I thought we could "solve" it and grow both: Keep the large customers and make the small ones profitable through automation and self-service.

We launched an e-commerce project with a webstore where customers could select, order, and pay for services online. In theory, this would reduce the cost to serve and allow us to grow that segment again.

In practice, it did neither. We didn't grow revenue from the segment, and we spent more money than before trying to fix it—it cost us time, people, and attention that should have been used elsewhere. It took about three years and plenty of frustration before we finally admitted it was a mistake and pulled the plug. Classic sunk cost.

The core lesson isn't whether e-commerce is good or bad, or whether small business can be profitable—there are many companies doing that successfully. The lesson is that when you have limited time and resources, you can't solve every problem. You have to choose which 20 percent to focus on, and you must be willing to say no to the rest.

So, in summary, good decision-making in a start-up means prioritizing what to work on, looking at decisions from different angles, and having the discipline to say no, even when it hurts your pride.

Next in the toolkit: continuous improvement.

5.4 Skill 3: Continuous Improvement

Continuous improvement is a well-known concept in business. There are many books and methods with fancy names—Kaizen, Six Sigma, Lean—all aimed at the same basic goal: make things better, little by little, all the time.

At Blue Wireless, I made continuous improvement part of staff onboarding. I reminded new joiners that they effectively had two jobs: "First, do your job. Second, make the company better." Over time, this mindset became one of our four core values: We evolve together.

In a start-up environment, applying continuous improvement comes with a few challenges.

First, while you may want perfection, you are limited in time, money, and attention. So, you constantly face three questions:

- Where do we start?
- When is something "good enough" for now?
- When is it time to improve the next area?

My personality is that of a generalist with an "80 percent is good enough" mindset. I can handle many topics reasonably well, but I'm not a specialist in any one area. I also have a fair amount of patience and can work on problems for weeks or months, but eventually I lose interest and want to move on.

Joop's character is more technical and perfectionist, which is essential in network operations. Internet Protocol networks don't work if you configure them "80 percent correctly." With customers expecting 99.9 percent uptime and smooth performance, every detail matters.

Both traits have advantages and risks. If you accept 80 percent everywhere, some parts of the business may fall apart. If you aim for 99.9 percent everywhere, you'll get stuck and never progress.

Another challenge is recognizing whether you're actually making progress. Looking at numbers—financials, volumes, delivery times—sounds logical, but there are issues:

Numbers only tell part of the story. They don't fully capture how your team is maturing, how your reputation is growing, or how robust your processes are. Those are hard to quantify.

When you're small, statistics can be misleading. In the early days, we tried measuring service levels like delivery times and uptime. Telecom is full of service-level agreement metrics, so we thought we should produce similar benchmarks. But when you deliver thirty new services in ten countries in a month, each one is different. One month we delivered a service in Indonesia in seven days and later one in Japan in eighteen days. Which is better? It depends on the location, urgency, and customer expectations. In both cases, the customers were happy.

On top of that, you often lack the systems to produce good data anyway. You haven't automated enough, so your numbers are incomplete or unreliable.

So how do you gauge progress? One simple way is to *look back one year.*

Look at pictures, presentations, sales materials, emails, even the office layout from a year ago and ask: How did we look? What were we doing? What were customers asking then? The difference is often huge.

Our monthly billing run, printing out invoices, Singapore, 2018

It's like watching your children grow. You don't see much change day by day, but when your phone shows you a photo from "this day one year ago," the difference is obvious.

I had one picture pop up of two of our early finance staff sitting behind a desk with a huge stack of letters and envelopes. They were printing each invoice by hand, putting them into envelopes, sticking stamps on, and taking them to the post office. On the way back, they'd stop by the bank to deposit checks before the 3 PM cut-off time. It looks archaic now, but that's how we did it.

We stopped paper invoices and checks long ago, but this kind of progress doesn't show up in financial reports or network uptime charts. Yet it's very real.

Continuous improvement in a start-up is partly about numbers but just as much about regularly looking up and looking back at where you came from and appreciating how far you've come.

5.5 Skill 4: Time Management

Next in the entrepreneurial toolkit is time management. You have limited time, potentially thousands of things you could or should do, and, hopefully, a life outside work. Or does that have to be sacrificed as well?

The movie *Everything Everywhere All at Once* (2022) captures that feeling of overload brilliantly. If you haven't seen it, it's worth a watch—though you may question whether spending two hours on a movie fits your time management goals?

In modern work, the line between work and personal time is already blurry. As an entrepreneur, it almost disappears. When do you start? When do you stop? Do you work days, nights, weekends?

I have to disappoint you if you're expecting heroic stories of "sleeping in the office, surviving on cold pizza, saving the day at 4 AM" stories. From day one at Blue Wireless up to ten years later, our story was more about consistency than drama. Just like fitness, you don't reach your goals with a few massive workouts. It's the daily grind that does it and a sixty-hour week was and is normal, and we got used to it.

My routine was fairly old school. I'd come into the office around 8 to 9 AM, turn on the computer, maybe clean some dishes, make a coffee, and start going through emails. I'd work until 6 to 7 PM. After dinner, there were often a few more hours of work, and occasionally a truly late-night session until 1 AM.

In the early years, Saturday was a standard workday for me. Joop and sometimes colleagues dropped by. Saturdays were for things we couldn't finish during the week: quiet work, tidying up, small office improvements, vacuuming, and cleaning—before we could afford a cleaner.

We made our offices places we wanted to spend time in: good coffee, music, a relaxed vibe, and, yes, some gins and wines. We spent a big part of our lives there, so it had to feel good.

When we traveled, we often did it over weekends or on red-eye flights to save on hotel nights and maximize working days. Where we could, we combined trips with visits to family or friends or short vacations. Nothing longer than a week, and we always kept our calendars synchronized, so that if one of us took a break the other was fully available.

Interestingly, I never felt that my family or social life suffered too badly. The area that usually suffered was my private "me time." There wasn't much of it, so I turned chores into me time: Saturday was perfect for that.

Spending some precious "me time" on Saturdays at the office.

The only thing that became mentally draining over time is that your brain never really switches off. Whether you're in the office or at home, the business is always running in the background of your mind. It becomes a permanent, never-ending puzzle.

That's the emotional side. On the practical side, you still need a simple system to handle the chaos: meetings, calendar, inbox. This depends a lot on personality, but here's what worked for me.

I used email as my main way to structure my actions and work. It gave me an overview of what was going on in the business. I had folders for major projects and topics and, yes, I let my inbox drive my day. Many experts say you shouldn't, but it worked for me.

The method I've used for years, and still use daily, is the Four *D*'s:

- **Delete**. At least half your mail is not important. Make a conscious effort to delete it. Don't just read and leave it sitting there, staring at you. You don't need to keep a record of everything ever said. And if it turns out to be important, there's always a sender who can resend it.
- **Do**. If something requires action and it can be done quickly, do it immediately. Many things only take a few minutes. As the organization grows, a large part of your job is giving approvals, making decisions, giving input. Do it fast. For nonstrategic stuff, don't overthink it. Keep moving. I often don't even prioritize among the "dos"; I just work through them in sequence.
- **Delegate**. As your team grows, more and more tasks can be handed off. Delegation isn't just "downwards" to subordinates; it can be to partners, peers, or external suppliers—whoever is best placed to handle it. The hard part is giving enough context and instructions. You'll always feel that you could

do it better yourself (and often you can), but you have to let go.
- **Defer.** My least favorite category, but sometimes necessary. Some matters need more time: You're waiting for information, you need to think, or you simply don't know yet. I leave these in my inbox and try to keep that list to half a page, roughly ten to twenty emails I'm actively working on.

To avoid being driven only by other people's priorities, I also email myself. My own tasks then sit in the same inbox, next to external mail, and I see everything in one place.

Personally, I'm not a fan of being driven by chat tools like Microsoft Teams or Slack. They can be useful, but constant pop-ups are distracting. That's personal preference though. Whatever tools you use, the key is to stay organized, because the amount of work grows with the business.

Time management for an entrepreneur is not about finding a magical schedule. It's about accepting that you'll work a lot, choosing a system that fits your style, and using it consistently so you don't drown.

Now for the final and most important tool in the kit: creativity.

5.6 Skill 5: Endless Creativity

Staying resilient, solving problems, improving things, juggling your time—one skill cuts through all of these: creativity.

Creativity is simply finding new ways to do things: better, faster, cheaper, easier, funnier, or just different. Sometimes we used creativity to solve real problems. Sometimes we did things just because we could.

I don't know if creativity is a personality trait or a learned skill, but I do know one thing: It's contagious. With Joop and me leading from the front with crazy ideas, we encouraged people to take risks, try new approaches, and accept that failure was absolutely an option.

Here a few stories of where creativity really came through.

Creative Marketing

Marketing is often the easiest place to be creative. In the early years, as mentioned earlier, we practiced a kind of guerrilla marketing and broke some conventions, and that spirit stayed with us later too.

One marketing stunt came from customers questioning whether our routers would survive the heat of Singapore. Many IT people came from corporate environments where the equipment lives in air-conditioned server rooms. We wanted to place routers where the 4G/5G signal was best, often in unair-conditioned spaces or outdoors. Our supplier, Cradlepoint, made rugged, heat-tolerant devices, but "it says so on the box" isn't always convincing.

So I grabbed a simple kitchen toaster oven. To make a demo video, I put the router in it, heated it up to around 100°C, then connected it to a laptop to show that it still worked fine. And it did. In services, seeing truly is believing, and you have to make things tangible or visible.

Router in the oven, notice the tongs, Singapore, 2017

Our marketing as a small company often punched above its weight. We took the "blue" theme to extremes (including blue wine), played online with memes, launched "bring a friend" promos, and implemented other ideas that went right up to the edge of what's normal in B2B (business-to-business) marketing. Fun, a bit cheeky, and memorable.

Creative Business

Running a small business gives you the feeling of being David in a world of Goliaths: You're at a disadvantage compared to the big and established guys, often you need to take risks, and, where needed, you bend the rules a little to even out the odds again, especially once events happen that you can't influence. The Covid-19 period brought such events upon us. Governments around the world overreacted with mandates, closures, surveillance, and more at a scale unseen in decades. While I was personally outraged about the government overreach during that time, we had a bigger purpose: building Blue Wireless. Resisting the government in Singapore was not a battle one should try to fight.

So, we abided by the rules and kept our head down and masks on. At some point during this period, closures were mandated for all offices, schools, etc., except for those businesses providing critical services in areas such as food, electricity, and telecommunications. While this was certainly meant for large telcos, I appealed on behalf of Blue Wireless with the regulator for exemption on the grounds of being an "essential" business providing Internet access. Although we were a small start-up of twelve people, we miraculously received approval, and we continued our work in the office as before. This kept not only the business going but also reinforced our reputation with customers that no matter what happens, Blue Wireless can be relied upon.

And as government grants became available to support businesses that were impacted by the Covid-19 regulations, we also took advantage of them. In the Netherlands, the procedure was such that any business that suffered severe revenue reduction could apply and receive government funds, but the actual proof of decreased revenue would only have to be supplied afterwards, in fact only a year later. And while we were growing our revenue steadily in the Netherlands, we applied for the funds (always be raising) and started the payback a year later once it was time to submit the numbers.

Masked and distanced (for the photo), Singapore, 2020

In both cases, we stayed within the law, but we pushed it to our maximum advantage, all with a greater purpose: The business needs to succeed. When under threat, one gets creative and leaves no stone unturned.

Creative Engineering

As we progressed, we did installations in all kinds of locations. Standard routers and antennas are designed for standard offices. Our customers wanted connectivity at wind farms, ships, fish farms, outdoor events, lighthouses—you name it. So, our engineers returning from the field started tinkering. They created custom boxes, transport cases, brackets, and power cables tailored to these environments. A whole internal language developed.

Antennas became "bunny ears" or "lightsabers." Our Wi-Fi event kits became "Big Brothers" and "Little Brothers."

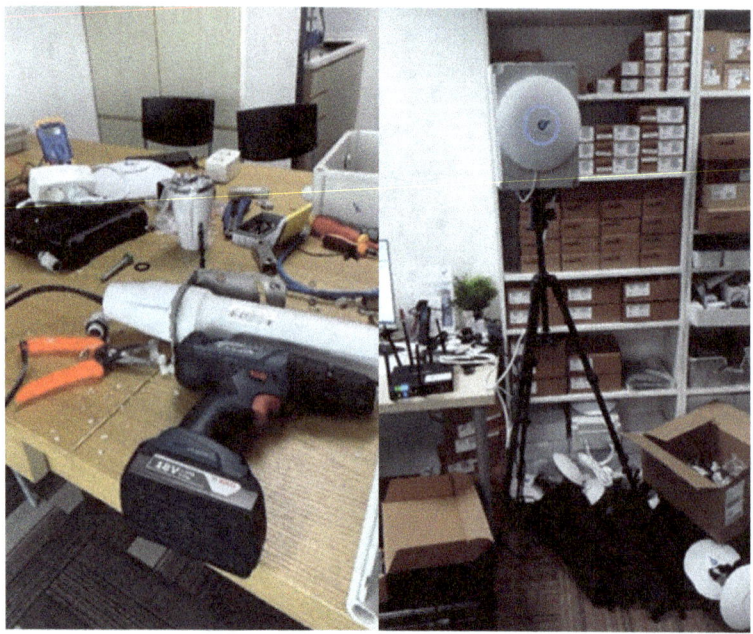

Creating "Big Brothers," Singapore, 2018

It was engineering, but it was also playful and creative. That spirit made tough jobs more fun and made our solutions more robust.

Creative Operations

Our promises to customers were often ahead of our actual capabilities, especially regarding local installations in many countries. At first, we operated only from Australia and

Singapore but promised "full service in sixteen countries across Asia Pacific." Later we expanded to seven countries, but we were servicing more than eighty countries. Getting equipment there was one thing, finding people to install it was another.

So, we got creative:

- First, we tried normal couriers. This was tricky because the equipment could be delayed by customs, approvals, and import taxes. Sometimes we described items as "household goods" or split shipments across couriers to increase the chance that something got through.
- Alternatively, we used colleagues, friends, and family as couriers. Many had slightly nervous moments at customs when asked if anyone had given them something to carry.
- We built a network of installers from the people we knew from our careers, plus friends and family. While the industry standard was a "Cisco-certified engineer," we often worked with what we jokingly called "sneaker boys": anyone nimble enough who could follow instructions over WhatsApp.
- If nothing else worked, we made a business trip or even a mini-holiday out of it and did the installs ourselves. It guaranteed quality and gave us a chance to see real-life conditions firsthand.

In the summer of 2020, we received a big batch order for a retail chain in Germany. We had to install at dozens of sites in a few weeks, far above our normal capacity. We took the order anyway and split the work among the three of us based in Amsterdam, turning each route into a small road trip.

I happened to be visiting my mother in the Netherlands and had promised to spend time with her, so I asked if she fancied a road trip through Germany. She loved the idea.

Installation tour, Germany, summer 2020

Over a week, we drove from Amsterdam to Cologne, Bonn, Koblenz, Stuttgart, Munich, and back, stopping at multiple sites each day. Since these were retail outlets, there was usually a German "Konditorei" nearby.

My mother would enjoy coffee and cake while I did the install. An hour later, we'd drive to the next one. In a few weeks, we finished all the sites, had a happy customer, and I had a happy mum and some great memories.

Jethro and Patrick packaging suitcases, Haarlem, the Netherlands, 2020

We were also creative in packaging. Initially, we shipped equipment in regular cardboard boxes. When we landed a complex order for installations on merchant ships, those boxes were not strong enough, not easy to carry on board, and prone to damage.

So, we sourced large-wheeled suitcases instead. The seafarers could keep them for personal use afterwards. We also filled them with Dutch *stroopwafels*, so they got a sweet surprise upon opening.

Our blue bus—with yet another slogan: "We're going wireless, where are you going?" Amsterdam, 2022

Sometimes creativity wasn't even problem-driven; we just saw opportunities. One friend had an old camping bus inherited from his late father and didn't know what to do with it. Fresh from the Germany road-trip experience, I saw the potential for a multipurpose Blue Wireless bus: a mobile unit to send engineers across Europe, fully connected and loaded with routers.

We wrapped the bus in our signature blue, and it became a multipurpose tool: a marketing vehicle, a support van for installations, and even a holiday bus for staff trips across Europe.

The list of creative, funny, and innovative things we did over the years is long and impossible to fully cover here. But one thing is clear: Creativity was not a side show. It was one of the foundations of Blue Wireless.

If resilience, decision-making, continuous improvement, and time management are the engine and structure of an entrepreneurial journey, creativity is the spark that keeps it exciting and helps you punch above your weight.

Anyone who wants to build a business needs to tap into that superpower!

Key Learnings

- As an entrepreneur, you need a blend of different skills; some are essential to have right from the start, some you can learn along the way.
- Resilience is not about never struggling but about bouncing back and making habits—using humor, perspective, and small rituals to keep going when the problems pile up.
- Good decision-making in a start-up starts with prioritization, looking from multiple angles and having the courage to say no, even when you've already invested time and money.
- Continuous improvement works differently in a young company: You rarely have perfect data, so you often rely on simply asking, "How do we look compared to a year ago?" to see your progress.
- Time is your scarcest resource; you need a simple, consistent system to manage your inbox, your calendar, and your energy—while accepting that the business will live in your head 24/7.
- Creativity is not a luxury add-on but an essential tool: from scrappy marketing stunts to hacked-together hardware, fresh ideas help you punch above your weight.

6 THE ART OF THE EXIT

Begin with the end in mind.

6.1 Why Sell?

Why sell something you've poured your heart and soul into? Something you've spent years of your life on, too much money, and plenty of blood, sweat, and tears?

It's an essential question, and it probably brings you back to an earlier one: Why did you start your venture in the first place? What was driving you at the start and during all those years? What are you trying to prove? And to whom?

Frankly, I've never been able to fully answer that even for myself. I just felt a strong desire to create something, to show I could do it, and to build something bigger than myself. And at some point, a sale became part of that process—a way to "finish the story."

Having gone through a sales process, I now see a few key reasons why you might want to sell—and also some reasons why you might not.

Reasons to sell:

- **Money.** The obvious one. A successful exit can result in a significant payout, sometimes at once, sometimes over time. That can be life changing (for better or worse). It raises big questions like what is the business really worth, and how much is "enough"? More on that later.
- **Peace of mind.** Exiting lets you "de-risk" your life and finally get to a feeling of safety: pay off loans, stop worrying about burning through your savings, and step back from being responsible for absolutely everything. Putting down the bricks for a while can

be an immense relief and allow you to recover some lost time, reduce stress, and maybe finally take that vacation properly.
- **Satisfaction of completion.** Besides relief, there is huge satisfaction in bringing a venture to a successful end. It's like climbing a mountain and making it safely back home. You did it. You can be proud of what you built and of the (hopefully) positive impact you had on others along the way.
- **Reputation.** Many people start a business; relatively few bring it to a successful exit where they walk away intact and are financially rewarded. If you do succeed, your name goes onto a small list. That can open doors for even bigger things or if you want to start another venture again.

But what you risk losing when selling:

- **Work satisfaction.** Creating your own business means designing your own job: what you work on, how you work, where you work, and with whom. That daily sense of control and meaning is very hard to match in a regular job. Giving that up can be one of the hardest parts of a sale. Where do you go from there? It's tough to go back to following instructions like a salaried employee.
- **Camaraderie.** It really does feel like a band of brothers and sisters: cofounders, early employees, and partners, all fighting as one from start to finish. You've been through good times and crises together. Letting go of that tribe is painful. You've been the underdog fighting the big guys—and now you might suddenly become part of them.

- **Your network and position.** Over the years you build a strong network and a reputation as a leader in your niche. When you sell, but especially if you leave, your formal position ends and with it a lot of those day-to-day industry interactions with customers, suppliers, and partners. Some of that can be reused for a new venture, but it's not the same.
- **Your purpose.** This is probably the hardest one. Your entrepreneurial journey gives your life a very clear sense of purpose, day in and day out. The moment you exit, that purpose changes or disappears. It leaves a void that takes real soul-searching to fill. "What now?" is not a small question.

All these points assume you actually have a choice about whether to sell. Plenty of founders don't have that luxury. They have to sell, exit, or even liquidate the business. It's not by choice, but because they run out of money, run out of energy, have cofounder conflicts, or face health problems that make continuing impossible.

But in the case of Blue Wireless we did have a choice. There was financial pressure, but we were never in a position where we were forced to sell. And as we're further getting into the mindset that a sale would happen in the years ahead, we start to prepare ourselves and the business for it.

Dr. Stephen R. Covey, in *The 7 Habits of Highly Effective People*, wrote: "Begin with the end in mind." It's useful advice for many aspects of life, but it's absolutely crucial if you plan to exit your business one day.

For an investor or buyer, one key question matters above all: Can this business continue to thrive without you? If the company would collapse the day you walk out, why would anyone invest serious money into it?

"Thrive" can mean different things to different buyers—some want growth, some want cash flow, some want technology or geography—we'll get into buyer types shortly. But the principle is the same: buyers pay for a business, not for you personally.

In that sense, you should think about your future buyers almost like customers: understand their needs and then build your company in a way that creates maximum value for them. In the process, you create maximum value for yourself. And like with customers, there is a sales process: generate interest, qualify serious prospects, negotiate, and close.

But before getting into the tactics and mechanics of a sale, you need to get yourself mentally ready. As a founder, you become incredibly emotionally attached to the business and to the people who helped you build it. For Joop and myself this was certainly true.

It's like raising a child from birth to adulthood. You go through ups and downs, sacrifices, and hard decisions together. But as a 'parent', your job is to make sure the company can stand on its own and survive in the world, with a potential new partner (owner), and needing you to take a step back. Letting go hurts—but it's part of the natural cycle and when it works, it's hugely satisfying to see the company you founded doing well in its next phase without you.

6.2 Four Ways to Sell a Business

When exiting a venture as an entrepreneur, there are roughly four main paths, each with its own characteristics.

1. **Trade sale.** Selling to another company in your industry is generally seen as one of the best options. This is often called a "trade sale." You speak the same "language" when it comes to products, customers, and markets, which makes discussions easier. There are usually clear opportunities for synergy: cost savings by removing overlap and revenue gains from combining suppliers, product portfolios, sales channels, and marketing. Those synergies can justify a higher valuation, because the combined business is worth more than the two separate parts.
2. **Private equity.** Firms invest in private companies to generate returns for their own investors. They are similar to venture capital funds, but usually come in later, when companies are more established and often when founders are looking for a (partial) exit. They typically hold their investment for a few years, then exit by selling to another investor, to a strategic buyer, or via a public listing. In this category, you can also include large, private investors or family offices who buy a significant stake.
3. **Public offering.** You can list your company on a stock exchange, which allows shares to be bought and sold publicly. It has become somewhat easier for smaller firms in recent years, but the hurdle is still high. You need scale, strong governance, audited

financials, and a credible growth story. Even after you list, you still need actual buyers. Often that means convincing institutional investors (funds, asset managers) to invest in your stock.
4. **Run for cash.** The final option is not to sell at all but to put a management team in place and pay yourself from the cash flow. Taking money out of the business for yourself often turns it into more of a lifestyle business: less money available for investment, slower growth, but a steady income. There are many creative versions of this: management buyouts (where staff borrow to buy shares), partial sales, or long, gradual handovers.

For Blue Wireless, the most realistic option was a trade sale as it allowed us to create most value and gave a clear exit path. Private Equity and Public offering would require many more years and Run for Cash wasn't the option for us – we wanted a clear payout at the end of the process.

But of course the question was: How much of a Payout do you need?

6.3 How Much is enough?

If you have not read *The Psychology of Money: Timeless Lessons on Wealth, Greed, and Happiness,* I strongly recommend you do, since as the title already states, money is more about emotions than it is about numbers. But let's get into the numbers and mechanics first before we get into the psychology of the sale.

For Joop and myself as founders the math of 'how much' (would we sell for) was quite simple – of course we wanted to maximize our payout after all these hard years, but how much money we really would need was simply the amount to pay off our debts and lead a comfortable life between now and the end of days. And comfortable was defined as the lifestyle we had before we started Blue Wireless, during our expat telco days. Combine them together, calculate the net present value and that would be our starting point.

But it wasn't just us, as our second group, our angel shareholders, also expected and deserved to be paid for their contribution. We assumed their math was broadly based on how much risk they had been exposed to for how long. The early investors has significant risk and expected to double their money or more, for later investors annual returns 10- of 20% per year would be adequate.

Thirdly, we needed to pay our company debts, stock options (SARS) and other expenses as part of the deal, all together a significant amount.

This simple bottom-up exercise gave us a good baseline of what the absolute minimum purchase price of the company needed to be if we could ever realize an exit. This number would be one part of the equation.

The other part would be what a prospective buyer would be willing to pay and here the leading metric is Enterprise Valuation (EV). Simply put what the company is worth driven by current P&L and Balance Sheet, but also by its future potential and the various risks. It's still a paper exercise and unless someone comes along and turns that into real money, as the buyer determines the ultimate worth of the company.

As we progressed through the years and our financial performance improved, the theoretical EV kept creeping up to the point where we felt it would cover enough to pay our angels investors, debtors and ultimately ourselves as founders. Time was an important element in this equation as while our EV improved over time and potentially could improve further as we continued, we didn't have enough free cash flow to realize our potential and our Angels were also stretched in providing ever more funds.

6.4 Determining the Right Time

So, besides the "why", "how" and "how much", the big question for us was really "when."

The actual decision by Joop and me to start a sales process was taken in the summer of 2022. We had been speaking with a Singapore private equity firm for a few weeks about potential new funding to fuel our ongoing expansion in Europe and US.

Those conversations were slow and frustrating. We felt our counterparts didn't really understand our industry, our concept, or our potential. They kept circling around market-share calculations and valuation models, and it just didn't click.

Around that time, Joop and I were travelling together to Kuala Lumpur when we received an invitation from two acquaintances in the management team of another global network service provider for dinner in Singapore. Our schedules were packed, and Joop was meant to fly back to

Sydney, but they were very persistent: It was urgent and there was "an opportunity" for us.

We changed our plans and flew back to Singapore to meet them. We didn't know the restaurant beforehand, but when we arrived, it was a Michelin-star fine dining place. That already made it clear: This was not a regular business dinner. Suppliers never took us out like that, and with customers we were always careful with budgets. This was full-on courtship. They pulled out all the stops.

The evening turned into night as we moved from wine to gin and tonics. They relentlessly pitched their idea of buying us out fully, throwing out valuation numbers and deal structures. They had clearly done their homework.

Initially we were resistant, but alcohol has a way of softening things. By the time we left, we ended with that classic line: "We'll think about it." They gave us forty-eight hours.

The next day, with the hangover still lingering, it was crunch time. Do we seriously want to entertain this or not? Numbers, emotions, plans, scenarios—all spinning around in my head: Was this the right time? If we sold too early, would we leave money on the table and never realize the full potential? If we passed and then ran into trouble later, would we regret missing this window? Would we end up as those desperate teenagers at the end of the night in a club when the lights come on and the party is over?

We decided we needed another night's sleep.

On the second day, the hangover was gone, our minds were clearer, and we had more distance. Without much drama, we both came to the same conclusion: The time was right. We should entertain their bid.

Their financial offer did meet the minimum EV rate that we had in mind, but wasn't overly generous. But what tipped the balance for us was the realization that a sale process would likely take a long time and secondly, even once the deal was done, we might still be working in the business for years.

Both turned out to be true.

We informed our "suitors" that we were interested, and the process began.

6.5 Selling for the First Time

As usual in our start-up journey, I was learning on the fly. I went straight to the big Kinokuniya bookstore in Singapore and bought a few books about selling your company and what to expect.

One book in particular, *Exit Right: How to Sell Your Startup, Maximize Your Return and Build Your Legacy* by Mark Achler and Mert Iseri, helped me understand the typical stages of an exit. In simplified form, there are five stages:

1. **LOI (letter of intent)**. A nonbinding document, usually from the buyer, outlining the high-level valuation and main terms under which they want to acquire the company. Negotiating this often takes a few weeks.

2. **Due diligence (DD).** The buyer (and their accountants and consultants) conducts an in-depth review of the company: financials, legal matters, customers, suppliers, staff, technology, contracts, you name it. This can take two to three months or more depending on complexity.
3. **SPA negotiation.** The share/stock purchase agreement (SPA) is the detailed contract that sets out the final conditions of the sale. It can easily be one hundred-plus pages and involves many hours of lawyers on both sides.
4. **Closing.** The moment when money changes hands, shares are transferred, and documents and systems are updated. This usually takes several weeks of preparation and a few hours of actual execution.
5. **Earn-out.** In growth companies, founders often stay on for a period after the sale, with additional payments tied to hitting agreed performance targets. This can run from one to three years, sometimes more.

Altogether, from the first serious conversation to final earn-out, the whole journey can easily take two to three years. That timeline helped confirm our earlier feeling: If we wanted to exit around a certain age or life phase, we needed to start the process well before that.

So there we were. For the first time, we weren't just selling services and ourselves; we were selling the entire company. We had an interested buyer, and we were willing sellers. What could possibly go wrong?

Quite a bit, as it turned out.

The first learning cycle started with the LOI. Negotiations spanned two weeks and went relatively quickly—in hindsight, too quickly. We didn't negotiate hard enough on the value and conditions, but at least it was a start.

Then came DD. That process was tough. It showed us how much work a serious sale actually takes and how underprepared we were. For two months, we lived in data rooms and spreadsheets: documents, checklists, forecasts, explanations, clarifications, and more explanations.

Together with a small team we pushed through all of it and felt we had done well. We survived the DD marathon and expected to move on to the next stage.

Instead, things went quiet.

Anyone who has worked in sales will recognize the pattern: A prospect calls saying they "need it urgently," but after receiving the quotation they go silent. Our potential buyer started delaying responses, asking for "more time internally," and generally dragging their feet on responses.

After several weeks of this, we finally received the answer: The deal was off. Reason: They weren't ready, priorities had changed, and they would not proceed. Our first serious attempt to sell had failed.

It was a major disappointment but also a valuable lesson. We learned a lot about our own numbers, our organization, and what a proper DD process looks like. And luckily, they were not our only suitor.

During 2022 and even before, we had regular approaches from companies wanting to talk about growth, financing, or potential acquisitions. One company I'd kept in friendly contact with was Wireless Logic. We knew them indirectly through Arkessa, one of our UK SIM providers they had acquired, and we knew they were backed by an ambitious private equity firm and were actively buying companies around the world.

During the first DD, Wireless Logic had contacted me again about a possible acquisition. I told them we were already in a process and couldn't talk. When the first deal fell apart, that door reopened. We shifted our attention to suitor number two: Wireless Logic.

This time there was no Michelin-starred dinner, no heavy wining and dining. Instead, we had a more straightforward business discussion, and we hit it off quickly with Richard Miller, the chief financial officer leading the process on their side.

We also decided to be more professional in our own approach. We asked the firm of our board member Chris Arscott, Titan Capital, to lead the negotiations and run DD on our side. That made a huge difference, for four reasons:

1. **Experience**. Chris ran an investment and finance firm and had real deal-making experience. He understood DD, lawyers, and closing procedures in a way Joop and I simply did not.
2. **Workload** The DD process overall was extremely taxing from a time and attention perspective and we could not have completed it without the work from Chris and his team as we had to continue to run the business daily. And at this stage, the business was running well, but we didn't want to make any mistakes that could jeopardize a good outcome.

3. **Professional image.** We now looked like a serious party with a proper team in place, not just two founders trying to manage a sale on the side while also running the business.
4. **Emotional distance.** Having Chris lead created space in negotiations. He could push and say no where needed, while Joop and I could maintain a good relationship with Wireless Logic for the long term.

With this setup, the second process went much smoother. From first serious discussion to signed SPA took around three months, which is considered very fast by industry standards.

The negotiations were tough but cordial, and we were both focused on making it happen. We learned to read each other's languages and distinguished important points from lesser demands. Richard referred to those latter points as "I wouldn't die in a ditch for this," which to this day cracks me up as it was such typical English humor. When we tried to make demands on certain points, he did not want to move on; he usually responded with "I'm sympathetic to your argument," which usually meant it was nonnegotiable. Over several weeks, we met the rest of the senior managers and personalities, and the working styles matched well.

The valuation we were able to achieve was significantly above the offer from our first suitor, although depended on future results which we had to achieve in an earn-out period.

At the same time, it was not only the negotiation with Wireless Logic but also "selling" the deal to all our angel investors. Some of the early investors had been waiting for years and, as they had invested at a low valuation, were ready to move on since it would result in a significant payout. Some of the later investors who came on board just twelve months prior at a much higher valuation preferred to hold out for a higher price over time. In the end, the sale was met with approval from all, which was important for us as we didn't want to have any disagreements or legal issues at the end.

By end of February 2023, we were approaching the finish line, and a new question emerged: How would other people react to the sale, especially to a 100 percent acquisition?

Up to that point, communication had been limited to a small circle: the board, shareholders, the finance team, and a few key staff. The rest of the company knew little or nothing. None of our customers or suppliers had any idea.

As we got closer to signing, we thought hard about the impact on our staff and especially our customers. Would customers trust us, just like they did in the early days when we pitched them our "crazy" wireless ideas?

We had built a strong reputation, but a lot of it was tied to Joop and me being the owners and taking personal responsibility. Would staff stay loyal to the company and the rest of the team, especially if we were "just" managers? Or if we eventually left?

We realized our personal involvement in the earn-out years would be crucial for bridging that trust gap and making the transition successful.

While lawyers were finalizing agreements and shareholders were voting, we prepared messages for customers and staff, draft announcements, and Q&As. We were trying to think through as many reactions and scenarios as we could and ultimately we prepared for most of the responses which would come our way.

6.6 Closing the Deal

And then the day arrived: Friday, March 3, 2023—signature day. Probably one of the most exciting, scary, terrifying, and exhilarating days of my life.

Signature day, Singapore, March 3, 2023

A complex, one hundred-page SPA document had been prepared by the lawyers, filled with clauses, conditions, and schedules. It required dozens of signatures, all wrapped up into a digital Docusign process to be completed within a few hours.

I sat in the meeting room of Blue Wireless Singapore, staring at the screen with the Sign button. There was no way back. Only forward.

With one click, it was done. Silence. No champagne. No balloons. No applause. Just a huge, quiet, internal "wow." It felt like a watershed moment and a strange anticlimax at the same time.

Looking back at my calendar and photos from that week, the only image that stands out from the day after is an airport. I was on a plane. It was literally back to work.

In the days that followed, reality started to sink in as we made announcements. Some of our larger GSP customers were shocked. Many uncomfortable conversations followed as we tried to calm their fears. They had seen this movie before: smaller providers acquired by larger ones, integration into the parent company, and the slow death of the acquired brand and culture.

In previous years, Expereo (my former employer, if you remember) had acquired several competitors. They took over their customers, absorbed their staff, and in the process many of those original companies effectively disappeared.

Our customers were afraid the same would happen to Blue Wireless. The acquisition meant less choice in the market, fewer truly independent players. We tried to assure them that this wouldn't be the case, and, thankfully, we turned out to be right.

Wireless Logic had different plans for us, and Blue Wireless became one of several operating companies under their umbrella, with a clear mission and identity. There was no push to kill our DNA or fully integrate us.

Blue Wireless joining Wireless Logic, late March 2023

Inside the company, staff reactions were mixed. Some were excited, some were hopeful, and many were anxious. The most common question was "What's going to happen to you guys? You're staying, right?"

We explained that it was "business as usual" in many ways, and that we actually had a lot of work ahead of us during the earn-out.

6.7 THE EARN-OUT

As part of the sale, Wireless Logic negotiated a two-year earn-out period—very common in growth companies where the founders are still central to running the business.

In some exits, founders dread the earn-out. They feel like they're hanging around, counting down the days until they can finally leave. For us, it was different. We wanted an earn-out, because we felt we weren't finished yet. We wanted to complete the job properly.

From a transaction and payment perspective, the earn-out meant that a significant portion of what we could earn depended on future performance. We would get paid based on hitting agreed targets.

The earn-out period is also when the new owners get to see whether what you promised during DD is real. If there are any skeletons in the closet, they usually appear in those first years.

We weren't too worried about skeletons—we had been truthful during DD—but the financial targets were steep. One main objective was to bring the company to consistent profitability. In the years before the sale, we were often borderline unprofitable: some good months, some bad, always needing more cash to fuel expansion and operations. Classic fast-growing, scale-up behavior.

The next two years were about growing up: becoming a "real" company that stands solidly on its own feet.

To hit our earn-out targets, we needed to do three things at the same time:

- keep growing revenue by selling and delivering more services;
- increase gross margin by reducing direct costs, mainly data and access expenses; and
- control operating expenses, especially our ever-growing workforce.

Not an easy combination.

On top of that, we now had a much larger parent company watching the numbers. These were the big unknowns:

Would the new owners support us or interfere too much? Would customers stick with us during the transition? Would staff stay motivated and committed under new ownership?

Those questions—and the way we tried to answer them—shaped the final part of our journey as founders of Blue Wireless.

Key Learnings

- Selling your company is never just about money; it is a balance of financial reward and peace of mind but also about giving up your purpose that comes with building your own company.
- A successful exit starts earlier: You have to build towards a company that can thrive without you, long before buyers appear.
- The sale process itself is a marathon of letters of intent, due diligence, contracts, and negotiations; it is demanding, deals can fall through, and having experienced guidance is crucial.
- An earn-out period is both a test and an opportunity: Prove the numbers you promised and reap the rewards.

7 WE MADE IT!

The day (and years) after.

7.1 Life Changing?

Looking back and reflecting on the period after the sale, both my working life and personal life changed far less than one might expect. In movies, exits are portrayed as explosive, life-altering moments: champagne showers, wild parties, and instant freedom once the first payment hits the bank account. Reality is far more subdued.

We always joked that we would know when we made it once we had our own T-shirt gun, Amsterdam, 2023

After the transaction, most of the time was spent taking care of others rather than us: reassuring staff, explaining the changes to customers, aligning suppliers and partners, making sure our angel shareholders were properly taken care of, and updating friends and family who all wanted to know what had really happened.

When we finally had time to look at our own finances, the initial focus was boringly practical: clearing debt. Over the years, we had accumulated mortgages, credit card debts, and personal loans, all in service of building the business. Paying those off became the priority. Settling those liabilities brought a much-needed sense of calm. One major, persistent stress factor disappeared: the feeling of being indebted everywhere, all the time. That burden weighs heavily on many entrepreneurs, often more than they care to admit.

What surprised me was what *didn't* change. Having more money in the bank did not reduce the drive to work hard. Nor were we suddenly motivated solely by the remaining earn-out payments we still had to earn. What kept us going was the clear sense that we were not finished with Blue Wireless yet.

There was personal pride involved, a desire to deliver on the mission we had committed to for the coming two years. And perhaps most importantly, we are creatures of habit. Eight years of intense work had conditioned us. Motivation matters, but habits carry you forward when motivation fluctuates. And so, we kept going.

7.2 Expansion Continues

Our mission after the acquisition was straightforward in theory but difficult in practice: continue to grow while becoming profitable at the same time. Any entrepreneur will recognize the tension in that statement. Growth demands investment, taking risk, spending money. Profitability demands restraint, saving cost.

We did the math carefully. If we kept executing well, we believed we could grow margins faster than expenses and reach the profitability required under the earn-out plan. The dilemma was how far to push new initiatives. Launching new products or opening in new countries typically hurts short-term profitability before it helps. The fastest way to improve the bottom line is often to do the opposite: stop investing, pause initiatives, and cut costs.

Some founders have gone to extremes during earn-out periods, laying off experienced staff—or even themselves—to boost short-term results. We consciously chose not to follow that path. Our pride and joy came from building the business further, not freezing it in time. So, during the earn-out years, we pushed ahead with several major initiatives to help grow the business to the next level. Four projects stand out in particular: the creation of a maritime team, the launch of enterprise sales, the expansion of our product portfolio with wireless Ethernet, and the addition of Starlink.

Back in the bus, winter 2024

Adding Starlink

By 2023, our customers were increasingly pushing us for broader wireless options. Starlink had emerged as the most-talked-about development in connectivity. While demand for LTE and 5G services remained strong, competition in that space was intensifying. Our coverage was still unmatched, and our service levels were industry leading, but we were no longer unique. The price pressure began to increase.

We also ran into physical limitations. Customers wanted connectivity farther and faster, often in extremely remote locations. LTE and 5G networks were not expanding fast enough in those areas, as mobile operators naturally focused on dense population centers. Despite creative antenna solutions and alternative designs, we could not ignore the growing impact of low-earth-orbit (LEO) satellite broadband.

In late 2023, we announced our intention to add Starlink to our portfolio and to deliver it in the same way as our existing services: fully managed, standardized, and available globally for enterprise customers. We worked in parallel on product development and negotiations. In March 2024, we became an authorized Starlink reseller, and in April we launched our Global Managed LEO service.

This was a breakthrough. Blue Wireless could now offer the best of both worlds: LTE/5G and LEO satellite connectivity, integrated into one global managed service. Once again, we were unique, creating a one-to-two-year head start on the competition.

Demonstrating Starlink during our launch party, Singapore, 2024

Frankly, without the acquisition by Wireless Logic, this would not have been possible. We lacked the corporate standing, volume commitments, and financial strength required. With Wireless Logic's backing, we led the negotiations and closed the deal on behalf of the entire group—a true litmus test of the partnership.

Within months, the majority of our global service provider (GSP) customers had signed up. Orders followed quickly. Within eighteen months, we delivered over one thousand services across more than fifty countries. Starlink fundamentally expanded what Blue Wireless could do and significantly increased our relevance to customers. We proved—to ourselves as much as to others—that we were not a one-trick pony. But it also introduced a new level of complexity, pushing the team beyond anything we had handled before. And this was not the only new thing.

Wireless Ethernet Services

Most people recognize an Ethernet cable: the familiar thick cable that plugs into a laptop or PC, delivering a stable connection.

But Ethernet is not really a cable, it's actually a layer 2 protocol developed in the 1980s and remains a preferred method for secure, controllable network access. It is widely used in wired networks, and our GSP customers were mostly buying Ethernet access for last-mile connectivity to their core networks. But most wireless services were often Internet Protocol-based, which didn't really match the setup of GSP networks. Ethernet over wireless was rarely available, but the technical advances in recent years changed that.

In 2024, we began developing a true global wireless Ethernet offering that used our regular wireless Internet access as a basis but used Ethernet virtual private networks across these links to connect to the core networks of GSPs. Developing this new capability required significant investment in networking equipment and countless hours of engineering trial and error. By late 2025, we achieved global readiness and added yet another capability to our ever-growing portfolio.

Blue Wireless Maritime

The creation of what we internally dubbed "Blue Wireless Maritime" started in 2024 with the addition of a company previously called M2MBlue, which was another acquisition by Wireless Logic a few years earlier. M2MBlue was a Dutch company that had operated for over two decades providing connectivity in the river cruise industry in Europe. Initially with 3G/4G connected routers and roaming SIM cards, it enabled Wi-Fi for passengers on board as they cruised along the Rhine or Danube throughout Europe. They already had started with the addition of Starlink as a connectivity method on customer ships and were on a similar trajectory in seeking the best of both worlds' connectivity for the twenty-plus vessels in their care.

The original founders of the company had left the year before. Wireless Logic was now looking after the company from the UK and the Netherlands by teams that had limited experience in managed network services compared to Blue Wireless.

So, in the summer of 2024, we started yet another dimension to the Blue Wireless business by bringing M2MBlue under our responsibility. The network services provided were complex, and financial performance was impressive—but the team was small (only fifteen people), and the business lacked spirit, process, and growth opportunities. But the match and synergies were evident: Both teams provided wireless network solutions for corporate customers. The M2MBlue team gave us a new dimension in the maritime segment.

First logo on the building, Arnhem, the Netherlands, Summer 2025

Enterprise Sales

Our go-to-market approach evolved several times over the years. We started with small, domestic customers and gradually moved toward global enterprises through GSPs. This strategy allowed us to focus on a single component—wireless access—while scaling efficiently across countries.

Our alignment with GSPs was a very successful strategy, as they held the key to enterprise customers. We could concentrate on delivering only one component (wireless access) and scale that to more countries, without having to get involved in the wider network complexities or expensive account management. The approach was a fruitful one because it allowed us to standardize products, create scale, and increase margin over time and get us to the run-rate we needed as we went through our acquisition process and earn-out targets. But it also left us vulnerable strategically for the long run, as over 90 percent of revenue came from a single product (fixed wireless) from a single segment (GSPs).

But with the addition of Starlink and the inclusion of the Blue Wireless Maritime team, our confidence and capabilities grew, and in summer 2024, we decided to strategically put this back on the map as a segment to pursue. So, we added new sales and service staff to develop the segment further and combined it with our new maritime customers into a new "Maritime and Enterprise" segment. The objective was not to compete with our GSP customers but to be able to fulfill more complex requirements in segments poorly served by GSP customers, such as energy, mining, and of course maritime.

All together, these new initiatives were well out of our two-year term scope when it came to simply reaching earn-out targets, but as entrepreneurs, we felt it was the right thing to get started for the long-term success of the business. And it laid the foundation for further success in years to come.

7.3 More Growth and Complexity

The period between 2023 and 2025 was not only one of growth and financial success but also of rapidly increasing complexity. It became clear that entrepreneurship was not just about adding—products, customers, people, revenue—but also about knowing when to stop, simplify, remove, or fundamentally reorganize parts of the business.

Looking back at that period, two headline numbers stood out. We grew from roughly 60 to 120 people. The monthly run-rate revenue increased from around 1 million Singapore dollars to more than 3.3 million Singapore dollars. Approximately a third of that growth came from the addition of Blue Wireless Maritime, the rest was organic. On paper, these were excellent results.

But size is only one dimension of growth. Complexity grew much faster. And there were other areas where we noticed significant changes:

One of the first things we noticed was the erosion of personal touch. In the early years, Joop and I knew everyone. We understood what motivated them, what frustrated them, and what they were working on. We were deeply involved, often too involved, but it worked at that scale. As the company doubled in size, that closeness became harder to maintain.

At the same time, our informal division of responsibilities stopped the scaling efforts we needed. Historically, I focused on the commercial side of the business: sales, marketing, product, finance, while Joop oversaw the technical side: operations, support, engineering, IT. That split had served us well for years. But with more products, more customers, and more people, the boundaries blurred and our way of "managing the world" became unsustainable.

Also, for years, we had relied heavily on constant travel: visiting offices, customers, partners, and teams across regions. Being physically present solved many problems before they escalated. But as the footprint expanded, this approach started to break down. You cannot be everywhere at once, no matter how many flights you take.

What we needed to sustain was a model that was no longer reliant on Joop and myself as the founders who knew it all and could be guided by a new management team.

And that set the stage for the most difficult question of all: Who will take over when we really exit the business?

7.4 LEADERS CREATE LEADERS

By end-2025, the earn-out period was officially completed, and we were down to the final financial formalities. But several months before, we knew already that our job wouldn't be done yet at that point. With the management of

Wireless Logic, we agreed to do one last 'push' for Blue Wireless: to concentrate on the next wave of leadership to make sure that we could leave the company behind and it would be ready for a future without us.

And yet again, we were starting with the end in mind— except this time the end would not include us. Our plan was based on two pillars: Localized decision-making and Succession planning.

Local Decision-Making

The centralized decision-making structure that Joop and I had practiced over the last eight years needed to change for a more localized approach and a proper global management team.

Having worked in large global companies before, I was familiar with the concept of "matrix" organization, which tries to blend the best of both worlds in terms of local decision-making and central control. It's not an easy task, as for every function, you can make an argument whether it should be managed locally or centrally, but as I write this, the new structure has been active for a good nine months and works successfully.

We decided on three regional managers—one for the Asia Pacific region, EMEA (Europe, the Middle East, and Africa), and the Americas—six functional managers with global responsibility, and one CEO; so a team of ten. For Joop and myself, it was an extra step to let responsibilities go and delegate even further. Joop's title changed from chief operating officer, which included all operational functions of engineering, delivery, and support to chief technology officer, which was focused on the technical aspects. My title of CEO remained as is, but I delegated more functions to the regional and functional managers.

Letting go is hard. After ten years of being on top of things, it is something you have to actively unlearn, as it does not come natural to a founder and entrepreneur.

The mindset change is the most difficult, as you need to stop doing and start delegating (remember the Four D's?) to get your team ready for the future. This means a few things:

First, accepting work that, in your own mind, isn't perfect. This for me was the hardest since over the years I became a stickler for the smallest things, from the stickers on customer packages to the coffee cup arrangements in the kitchen, always trying to "fix" things… After all these years "in the trenches," I need to rewire myself to look above it and wane myself off the problem-solving addiction

Second, it wasn't just delegating work but letting others make decisions and accepting that those decisions to be different than what you would have chosen. In some cases, it's letting others struggle to see if they can figure it out. In the end, if they were to run the business in the future, they would have to live with these decisions.

While I knew these things were necessary, mentally it felt wrong, like I was "taking it easy" or was dodging responsibility. But in the end, I believe it made the future leadership team stronger, and that was necessary for the final stage: succession

.

Succession Planning

What I have learned about succession planning is that it is not a one-to-one replacement of a person. You don't need another founder to succeed you, and you don't need to look for a carbon copy of yourself. It would be impossible to find anyway.

In early 2026, the task at hand was a big one: As a company, we had the potential to continue to grow significantly. We were doing roughly 25 million US dollars of annual revenue, which still put us on the lower end of a mid-size company. The next psychological number to meet would be 100 million US dollars, and this would be entirely possible but would take several more years to achieve with more hard work ahead. Standing at this crossroads of succession planning, I felt three major things had to happen:

1. We needed to continue to create more value for our global customers through further service development. Our customers continued to demand better: more reliability, faster service, more friction removed from our delivery and support processes. We were not good enough to truly excel in our field and service the customers of the future.
2. Significant automation was needed to keep the business model sustainable, both financially and operationally. At some point, you can't keep adding more people or trying to work harder; systems need to make things smarter. To be ready for the future, this would mean another overhaul of the systems that we previously built.
3. We needed to continue to grow, develop, and localize our global team of people, which would

remain our greatest asset and differentiator as a service company. Systems would need to do the operational tasks, but the innovation, customer service, and creativity to keep on developing the business comes from good people.

Together, this wasn't a simple checklist for the next quarter but a multiyear task. Such a task would require leadership from people that not just have adequate business experience but more importantly, possession of the Blue Wireless "grit" or DNA that was shaped over the years—the dealing with complexity, a mindset of service excellence, the focus on people, and someone who will "bleed blue" when needed.

Luckily, we didn't have to look far. Throughout the years we built an amazing team of people including several in the management team capable of leading the business. It turned out my last job as CEO was not to run the company but to be a leader to create new leaders. And with that last task the cycle of a founder truly comes to an end.

Key Learnings:

- *A successful exit should change the financial pressures in your life, but it doesn't change who you are or what drives you to do the day-to-day.*
- *After the exit and earn-out milestones are reached, discipline and habit matter far more than motivation or incentives.*
- *The earn-out is not just about the financial results—keep building the company for the future.*
- *More growth usually increases complexity, therefore keep updating the organization.*
- *The final task of a founder is not to run the company but to leave behind other leaders to take over.*

8 WHAT I HAVE LEARNED

Final Thoughts

So here we are, the final chapter. The writing of this book was a small journey by itself, with lots of learning on the fly like I did during the previous ten years and discovering many new things along the way.

Celebrating ten years of Blue Wireless, Singapore, August 2025

How do you distill ten years of building a business into a few lessons for budding entrepreneurs? What are the final takeaways about how to start, grow, scale, and exit a business? Is it cash flow, customers, margin, accounting, or product-market fit? With the writing of this book, I was able to reflect on the ride and its lessons, and they are more personal than business in nature. There is no single playbook or manual, and everyone's situation and journey is different. The following things stood out for me:

You Need Endurance

Yes, I brought telco experience, some starting capital, a professional network and business confidence at the start, but that wasn't the thing that made us successful. Nor was it the idea of "5G networking for corporates" or our superior technology. It was the endurance to keep going, to keep learning, to keep changing—to never give up. This truth has been proven many times: Many businesses don't succeed or fail because of good or bad ideas, but because the founders run out of steam. And you can't endure by just brute self-motivation, you have to create an environment that you love to come to, hire people whose company you enjoy, and turn your chores into habits; that way you can keep showing up. I believe we did.

You Need a Great Culture

"Customers will never love a company until the employees love it first" said business leadership author Simon Sinek, and it is true. The Blue Wireless culture has been a cornerstone of our success and continues to be the glue that keeps the team together. I gave the spark and set the example, but from there it grew over time through every person that joined and an accumulation of successes, failures, stories, parties, and ups and downs. It's what customers recognize, what differentiates us in the market, and what sets us apart from competition. It's our "secret sauce." I'm astonished sometimes how serious our staff take our Blue Wireless culture and actively live and defend it. For any entrepreneur, this is something you should cherish and cultivate whenever you can.

You Need Long-Term Goals

Sticking to the long-term success goals is key. For Joop and me, it was to build a proper global business, which would be sustainable and profitable and from which we could retire from. It's a big, ambitious goal when you're working in your spare bedroom, but set a long-term goal, break it up into smaller segments, and keep tweaking them once you get to the next level. Yes, we made short-term tactical decisions to survive and many adjustments along the way, but our long-term outlook was always the same, from the Asia Pacific to Europe to the Americas to global to exit. That was the master plan. Start with the end in mind and work backwards.

You Need to Let Go

In the early years, I was doing many things myself, not just because there were few alternatives, but I wanted to control each element. From the size of the storage shelves to the layout of our ordering form to the size of the logo, I went through it all, and it had to get done my way. Over time, I learned that I needed to let go but not just delegate—I had to actually start trusting others to handle it, allowing them to make mistakes to learn and grow. In the process, this shift would develop the next generation of leaders to take over the management of Blue Wireless. This portion has always been difficult for me, as many of my staff will attest.

There is a quote that states that "If you're the smartest person in the room, you're in the wrong room." Personally, I was that person for too long, and it was time to not be the smartest but the calmest.

You are Building Something Bigger than Yourself

My deeper motivation to create Blue Wireless was coming from this desire to create new things, build something, and test myself. Did I succeed? I believe so. But what I didn't fully realize and appreciate until now was that what I built wasn't for myself.

Yes, I started and nurtured Blue Wireless to maturity, but the company that exists today will live on and is carried by a team of people every day. The business created not just employment and good payouts for those who participated but also learning, growth, and inspiration for many. In that way, I believe that being an entrepreneur is actually a "noble" profession, and we need more dreamers and builders to create purpose for everyone.

So, to everyone who is thinking about taking the leap and starting something new—go for it! Onwards and upwards!

9 Thank You

This journey would have been impossible without you.

Joop

Blue Wireless would have been impossible without you. Simple as that. Your spirit, persistence, technical know-how, work ethic, humor, and espresso and alcohol tolerance are unmatched. We shared so many of the same beliefs, and you beat me to the office for so many mornings, the dishwasher already empty or the music already on by the time I arrived. Damn. You are one in a million. I loved how we found our balance, like married people learning to live with their differences because they know there is something greater than themselves. We did it.

My Wife

I know you are my biggest fan and so am I of you. While we argued about many things in life, we never did so about Blue Wireless; your support was unconditional. You not only believed in me and put up with my endless hours, but you pawned your jewelry, sacrificed your credit score, kept your sanity, and kept cooking for everyone. Love you.

Our Early Investors

Louis and Gary trusted us with their money when we still couldn't properly articulate what we were doing or how they would ever get it back. Many followed and invested as shareholders: Pinaki, Sean, Craig, Carsten, Ronald, Chris Arscott, Chris and Jee, Chris Acret, Jord, Kenn and Pla, Bill and HyunJoo, Deepti, and Andrew. Many also extended loans: Joost, Pauline, Andy, and others. You were patient and fair, and I'm relieved—and proud—that everyone got their money back, and then some. And to the early investors: You hit the investment jackpot. You earned it by trusting me and Joop.

Our First Joiners

I pursued **Syam** for many months to join me, and when he finally did, Blue Wireless went from zero to hero thanks to his relentless technical work. You defined many of the technologies and practices we still use today.

I will never forget the morning **Deepti** joined for her first day as a finance admin, and I asked her to come along on an install at a construction site. Her eyes showed equal parts amazement and terror as she thought, *"Where in God's name did I end up?"* But you stuck with me through all these years. Thank you.

Chin Tat became Mr. Blue Wireless from day one and is still today, even after leaving us for Singtel and Cradlepoint. Your enthusiasm and funky spirit were just what we needed during those early years.

Manju was the quiet powerhouse that powered the backend of Blue Wireless for many years and still is today the only person who knows every single detail. Amazing.

Cera, you joined as a young salesperson searching for purpose and developed into an ambitious businesswoman with an energy that wears out anyone. Incredible.

Many followed after that and many are still with us today: **Lyndon** and **Jon**, our Filipino power couple; **Adam**, who setup and grew our Malaysia business; and **Elvin**, who kept our sanity as we professionalized our products and processes.

Pieter, Wilmer, Patrick, Chico, and **Wouter,** who started very humbly in the Netherlands and laid the foundation for the biggest part of Blue Wireless in Europe—you made it happen.

Michael and Andrew, who pioneered the US and UK as we pushed westwards—you are amazing, and you brought in many more amazing colleagues who form the Blue Wireless as we know it today.

The Titan Team

Chris, you were always the smartest and most 'suited up' man in the room and your sharp eye and humor got us through the deal. Thanks to **Rob** and **Jeff** for the endless DD grunt work, without your patience we couldn't have closed the deal.

All Our Staff

To everyone working at Blue Wireless today: I thank and salute you. You carry forward the spirit of what we started. I am truly proud and humbled when I see how people embrace the culture, support each other, have fun, and so often put the company before themselves. You carry the torch now, and you have the opportunity to do amazing things—to learn, to create, to lead, and to discover what else you have in you.

Wireless Logic

Richard and Oliver, many people told us that they loved what we were doing, but you put your money where your mouth was and gave us the boost to take things to the next level. You believed we could achieve what we set out to do, and we believed you would give us the means and room to do it. We were both right. While I don't have many personal benchmarks for comparison, I believe this is how acquisitions should be done. **Simon**, thank you for applying a light touch in managing two entrepreneurs during their earn-out—giving us the space to do what we do best and support where we needed it.

Customers & Partners

I doubt that many of our first customers realized that they were among the first, but I certainly remember, as we were learning on the fly and always pretending to be bigger than we actually were. The first GSP we signed back in 2017 is still the largest today in 2026: **BT.** If we didn't have BT, we would not have been where we are today. Same is true for **Scape** (Australia). Without their early boost in work and cash flow, we could not have survived and developed.

The choice of **Cradlepoint** back in the early months was purely by chance (I was just Googling), but their technology and partnership became the foundation of our business for many years. So many other local installation partners across various countries trusted us with our crazy ideas and requests, but you helped us tremendously to become global, and you helped our customers when they needed it most.

Thank you all.

10 References

Interesting books, articles, and movies to explore.

Achler, Mark. *Exit Right: How to Sell Your Startup, Maximize Your Return and Build Your Legacy.* Lioncrest Publishing, 2022.

Coffey, Adam. *The Exit-Strategy Playbook: The Definitive Guide to Selling Your Business Paperback.* Lioncrest Publishing, 2021.

de Bono, Edward. *Six Thinking Hats.* Little, Brown and Company, 1985.

Glengarry Glen Ross, directed by James Foley (1992).

Greene, Robert. *The 48 Laws of Power.* Penguin Books, 2000.

Harnish, Verne. **Scaling Up**: *How a Few Companies Make It...and Why the Rest Don't.* rev. ed. Gazelles, Inc., 2022.

Holiday, Ryan. *The Daily Stoic: 366 Meditations on Wisdom, Perseverance, and the Art of Living.* Portfolio, 2016.

Housel, Morgan. *The Psychology of Money: Timeless Lessons on Wealth, Greed, and Happiness.* Harriman House, 2020.

Neff, Thomas J. *You're in Charge—Now What? The 8 Point Plan.* Crown Currency, 2007.

www.ingramcontent.com/pod-product-compliance
Lightning Source LLC
Chambersburg PA
CBHW050051230526
45470CB00004B/1488